INTERPRETING BASIC STATISTICS

A Guide and Workbook Based on
Excerpts from Journal Articles

Zealure C. Holcomb

Pyrczak Publishing

P.O. Box 39731

Los Angeles, CA 90039

CONTENTS

Notes:

INTRODUCTION

This book presents brief excerpts from research journals representing a variety of fields. The questions that follow each excerpt allow students to practice interpreting published research results.

The questions require students to apply a variety of skills including

1. locating specific information in statistical tables, figures, and discussions of results;

2. performing simple calculations to determine answers to questions not directly answered in the excerpts;

3. discussing the authors' decisions regarding reporting techniques;

4. describing and interpreting major trends revealed by data, including evaluating the authors' interpretations; and

5. evaluating procedures used to collect the data underlying the statistics presented.

Although the excerpts emphasize the "results" sections of the journal articles from which they were drawn, some information about procedures, such as sampling and measurement, are also included in order to put the results in context.

The appendices present four complete research articles so that students can study the structure of typical articles.

Some Assumptions Underlying the Development of this Book

A major assumption is that students will find materials based on actual research reports inherently more interesting than made-up examples that are often used in statistics textbooks.

It is also assumed that students will benefit by practicing with materials written by numerous authors; this allows them to see variations in the uses of statistics and in reporting techniques as they are actually used by practicing researchers.

Finally, it is assumed that a collection of complete research reports would produce too much material to be integrated into traditional statistics courses. Instructors of such courses are often pressed for time when covering just the essentials. Hence, this book presents brief excerpts to conserve instructional time.

Cautions When Using this Book

Students should be aware that the exercises are based on excerpts from journal articles. Although the excerpts are in the original authors' own words, many important points made in the complete articles were omitted for the sake of brevity. Before generalizing from the excerpts, such as in papers written for other classes, students should read the full articles, which are available in most large academic libraries.

Although the answers to most of the questions are either right or wrong, some questions may have more than one good answer because they ask for subjective interpretations or speculation. At first, some students are surprised to learn that the interpretation of data is not always straightforward; yet, it is precisely because of this circumstance that practice is needed in interpreting research results as they actually appear in journals.

A statistical guide at the beginning of each exercise provides highlights that help in the interpretation of the associated excerpt. The guides are not comprehensive because it is assumed that students using this book are enrolled in statistics courses in which theoretical and computational concepts are covered in detail in their textbooks. Thus, the guides should be thought of as reminders of basic points to be considered when attempting the exercises.

Finally, students will discover occasional inconsistencies between what is recommended by their textbook authors and the analysis and reporting techniques employed by the authors of the excerpts. Variations are permitted by journal editors, and the excerpts in this book will help students prepare for reading research reports as they actually appear in journals. When taking tests in class, however, students should always conform to the recommendations made by their textbook authors or by their instructors.

Notes on the Layout of this Book

To minimize page turning while answering the questions, each exercise begins on a left-hand page and most of the questions are on the facing right-hand page. A page for notes has been placed between exercises, which allows removal of a completed exercise that is being collected as homework without removing any portion of the previous exercise. The pages are perforated to permit easy removal.

Acknowledgements

I am grateful to Robert Morman of the California State University, Los Angeles and to Richard Rasor of the American River College for their helpful comments on the first draft of this book. I am also indebted to Holbrook Mahn and Patricia A. Steele for their editorial assistance.

Zealure C. Holcomb

EXERCISE 1

GIFTED CHILDREN'S FEARS

STATISTICAL GUIDE

Percent means "per one hundred." For example, if there are 1,000 residents in a town and 40% are Republican, then, on the average, 40 out of each 100 are Republican. To determine the total number of Republicans, multiply 1,000 by 0.40, which yields 400.

N or n stands for the number of cases or subjects.

To the right of the decimal point, the first numeral indicates the number of tenths, the second indicates the number of hundredths, etc. Thus, "6.7" is read as "six and seven tenths."

EXCERPT FROM THE RESEARCH ARTICLE

All students attended a Toronto public school for gifted children, had been previously identified as gifted, had an IQ of 130 or higher, and had been screened by a preschool admission committee consisting of psychologists, teachers, and the principal.

Each child was asked to respond in writing to the question, "What are the things to be afraid of?" The direct question, "What are you afraid of?" was not used since children might regard it as a form of criticism or be embarrassed by the responses and subsequently alter them.

The responses within categories were computed by grade level (Table 2). Comparison of fears across grades indicated that the most common fears of gifted students were categorized as Nuclear War–58.6%; Violence–55.7%; Miscellaneous–47.1%; Death–40%; and People–32.9%.

Table 2   Percentages of Fears by Grade*

Grade	Animals	People	Dark	Spooks	Natural Hazard	Machinery	Poison Drugs Alcohol	Death	School	Nuclear War	Violence	Misc.
4 (n = 10)	20.0	10.0	0.0	10.0	40.0	30.0	10.0	50.0	10.0	50.0	60.0	20.0
5 (n = 15)	40.0	73.0	46.7	40.0	13.3	26.7	26.7	26.7	6.7	33.3	60.0	66.7
6 (n = 15)	40.0	20.0	20.0	6.7	33.3	20.0	40.0	53.3	6.7	86.7	73.0	46.7
7 (n = 14)	28.6	50.0	28.6	0.0	21.4	14.3	21.4	21.4	42.9	64.3	57.0	57.1
8 (n = 16)	12.5	6.3	6.3	12.5	25.0	6.3	12.5	50.0	31.3	56.3	31.0	37.5
Total**	18.6	32.9	21.4	14.3	25.7	18.6	22.9	40.0	20.0	58.6	55.7	47.1

*Percentage of students who mentioned each category at least once.
**Total number of responses = 393.

SOURCE: Derevensky, J. & Coleman, E. B. (1989). Gifted children's fears. *Gifted Child Quarterly, 33,* 65–68. Copyright 1989 by the National Association for Gifted Children. Reprinted with permission.

QUESTIONS FOR EXERCISE 1

1. The percentages in Table 2 were rounded to the nearest (circle one)

   A. whole number.   B. tenth.   C. hundredth.   D. thousandth.

2. How many sixth-grade children responded?

3. What is the total number of children who responded?

4. What percentage of the fifth-grade children reported being afraid of the dark?

5. How many of the fifth-grade children reported being afraid of the dark?

6. How many of all children in all grades reported being afraid of death?

7. In addition to reporting the percentages for each category of fear, would it also have been desirable for the authors to report the numbers of cases (i.e., frequencies) such as the numbers that you calculated in response to questions 5 and 6 above? Explain.

8. In general terms, describe the developmental trend in fear of machinery (across grade levels).

9. In general terms, describe the developmental trend in fear of school (across grade levels).

10. The sum of the percentages across the first row (for fourth-grade students) is considerably greater than 100 percent. Speculate on the explanation for this.

11. The second footnote to Table 2 indicates that there were 393 responses. Is 393 the *sample size*? Explain.

12. If you were planning to summarize this study in a term paper on fears of nuclear war, would you mention the fact that all of the subjects were gifted? Explain.

13. If you were planning to summarize this study in a term paper on gifted children's fears, would you mention the sample size and origin of the sample? Explain.

14. Do you agree with the authors that it was better to ask "What are the things to be afraid of?" instead of "What are you afraid of?" Explain.

Notes:

EXERCISE 2

ENDING A CAREER IN A DECLINING INDUSTRY

STATISTICAL GUIDE

In random sampling each member of the population is given an equal and independent chance of being selected; this may be accomplished by drawing names from a hat or using a table of random numbers.

Demographics are background characteristics (i.e., variables) that are used to describe the subjects of a study. They are usually not the focus of the study. Examples of commonly used demographics are gender, age, and ethnicity.

Note that in the table below, dashes are used to represent percentages of zero.

EXCERPT FROM THE RESEARCH ARTICLE

A questionnaire was mailed to a random sample of 500 United Auto Workers retirees who had been employed in the Rouge auto plant in Dearborn, Michigan. All retirees were eligible for full pension benefits based on a combination of age and length of service. After a follow-up mailing two months later, about 40 percent returned the questionnaire. A comparison of the demographic characteristics of this sample with both U.S. Census data and other retired worker surveys suggests that this sample . . . reflects basic characteristics of auto workers as reported in the 1980 census (U.S. Bureau of the Census, 1980).

As Table 5 demonstrates, over two-thirds of those who retired at age 65 or older cited age as the primary reason for retirement, compared to one-tenth of the early retirees and less than one-fourth of those who retired between ages 62 and 64.

Table 5   Reasons for Retirement by Age at Retirement

Reason for retirement	Age at retirement		
	Under 62	Between 62-64	65 or older
Age	10.5	22.7	64.6
Ready to retire	10.5	48.9	14.6
Health problems	26.3	12.1	8.3
Plant closed	10.5	1.5	—
Benefits	10.5	3.0	—
Make way for younger workers	2.6	1.5	6.0
Bad work conditions/industry uncertainty	5.3	4.5	—
Family concerns	7.9	—	2.9
Enjoy life	7.9	1.5	2.1
Other	7.9	4.5	2.1
	100.0%	100.0%	100.0%
n =	76	66	48

SOURCE: Meyer, M. H. & Quadango, J. (1990). Ending a career in a declining industry: The retirement experience of male auto workers. *Sociological Perspectives, 33,* 51–62. Copyright 1990 by JAI Press, Inc. Reprinted with permission.

QUESTIONS FOR EXERCISE 2

1. What is the total number of subjects on which Table 5 is based?

2. Of the 76 subjects under age 62, how many reported that their reason for retirement was to enjoy life?

3. How many of the subjects who were 65 or older reported that their reason for retirement was because of bad work conditions/industry uncertainty?

4. For those subjects who were under 62, what was the least frequently cited reason for retirement?

5. In words (not numbers), describe the relationship between age at retirement and health problems as the reason for retirement.

6. In words (not numbers), describe the relationship between age at retirement and age as the reason for retirement.

7. Is the relationship between age at retirement and being ready to retire as a reason for retirement consistent across ages from the youngest to the oldest retirees? Explain.

8. Suppose that the authors had reported *only* numbers of cases in the table and had *not* reported percentages. (For example, in response to question 2 above, you calculated the number of cases for one cell.) Would such a table be more or less useful than the table actually presented? Explain.

9. The authors gave the table both a number and a title. Was this a good idea? Explain.

10. The authors mailed the questionnaire to a random sample of the population. In light of the response rate, do you believe that it was important for the authors to mention the demographic characteristics of those who responded? Explain. (Note: In the complete article, the authors describe the demographics in more detail than given in the excerpt.)

11. In the complete article the authors examined the relationship between age of retirement and several variables in addition to the reasons for retirement. What other variables might you wish to examine?

Notes:

EXERCISE 3

STUDENT ACCESS TO GUIDANCE COUNSELING

STATISTICAL GUIDE

A proportion is a part of one (1). For example, a proportion of .2 stands for two-tenths of one. The highest possible proportion is 1.00, and the lowest is 0.00.

To convert a proportion to a percentage, multiply by 100. For example, .2 x 100 = 20 percent.

To review percentages, read the statistical guide for Exercise 1.

EXCERPT FROM THE RESEARCH ARTICLE

[The] issues were investigated using *High School and Beyond* (*HS&B*), a large study of high schools and their students . . . . Our major analyses have been restricted to the 9,471 public high school students for whom there was test, questionnaire, and transcript file information.

One way of investigating how students arrive in their curricular tracks is simply to ask them. Such a query was included in the (*HS&B*) base-year questionnaire; we present the results in Table 1. More students report being assigned to their tracks than any other option.

Table 1   Proportions of public high school sophomores in each curriculum track reporting methods of track placement

Method of track placement	Curriculum track		
	Academic	General	Vocational
Only one offered	.02	.03	.03
Assigned	.33	.43	.37
Chose alone	.25	.23	.25
Chose with counselor*	.28	.19	.21
Chose with others	.13	.11	.13

*Includes four categories: chose with counselor only; chose with counselor and parent(s); chose with counselor and friend(s); chose with counselor, parent(s) and friends.

We have seen in Table 1 that students in the three curriculum tracks report different degrees of counselor assistance in placement into those tracks, with more of those in the academic track reporting counselor contact.

SOURCE: Lee, V. E. & Ekstrom, R. B. (1987). Student access to guidance counseling in high school. *American Educational Research Journal, 24,* 287–310. Copyright 1987 by the American Educational Research Association. Reprinted by permission of the publisher.

QUESTIONS FOR EXERCISE 3

1. What proportion of the students in the vocational track reported being assigned to that track?

2. What percentage of the students in the vocational track reported being assigned to that track?

3. In which curriculum track did the largest proportion of students choose their track with counselors?

4. What is the size of the difference, expressed in proportions, between those in the academic track and those in the general track who chose their tracks with counselors?

5. What is the size of the difference, expressed in *percentages,* between those in the academic track and those in the general track who chose their tracks with counselors?

6. What is the sum of the proportions in the column for the general track?

7. Speculate on why the sums of the proportions in the three columns do not equal one (1).

8. The authors state that "more students report being assigned to their tracks than any other option." Is this statement consistent with the proportions presented in Table 1? Explain.

9. Is it possible to determine from these results the proportion of students who chose their tracks with the assistance of both counselors and parents? Explain.

10. Comment on the adequacy of the sample size underlying the proportions reported.

11. If you were preparing a summary of this research to present to parents at a PTA meeting, would you report proportions or percentages? Explain.

12. Are there any dangers in collecting the data presented here by simply asking students how they arrived in their curricular tracks? Explain.

13. In your opinion, are there any potential methodological problems in analyzing data collected as part of a previous study? (For example, the authors used data collected for the *HS&B* study in their study.) Explain.

14. Keeping in mind that the titles (i.e., captions) of tables should be brief, comment on the adequacy of the title given to Table 1.

Notes:

EXERCISE 4

WOMEN'S CHANGING WORK ROLES

STATISTICAL GUIDE

Figure 1 is a time series graph, that is, a line graph showing changes over time. The dots were connected to help the reader visualize the trend(s) over time.

EXCERPT FROM THE RESEARCH ARTICLE

Unless otherwise noted, the source of the statistics described in this section is the edited volume, *Women's Changing Role* (Foster, Siegel, & Jacobs, 1988), which is a compilation of statistics provided by the Bureau of Labor Statistics, National Center for Health Statistics, Bureau of the Census, and National Science Foundation. As Figure 1 shows, rates have increased throughout the century. At the turn of the century, the rate was 19.7%, but in 1970 49.2% of the women in this age group were in the labor force. The 1988 rate of 66.9% of women aged 25 to 64 (Green & Epstein, 1988) is expected to increase to 80.8% by the year 2000, with 66 million women projected to be in the labor force at that time.

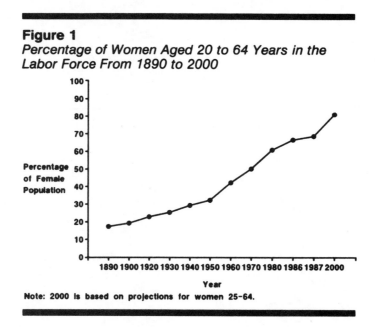

Figure 1
Percentage of Women Aged 20 to 64 Years in the Labor Force From 1890 to 2000

Note: 2000 is based on projections for women 25-64.

As with long-term trends, in the last 10 to 20 years all demographic groups of women have not experienced the same magnitude of increase in labor force participation. Since 1975 the rate of married working women has increased from 44.4% to 54.6% in 1986. This rate increase is substantially larger than the changes for divorced women (72.1% to 76.0%), never married women (from 56.8% to 65.3%), and widows (23.9% to 19.3%) across comparable years.

Among married women, the women with young children have shown the most dramatic increase in labor force participation. About 54% of married women whose youngest children are under the age of six are in the labor force compared with only 30% in 1970. The comparable figure for 1960 was 17%.

SOURCE: Matthews, K. A. & Rodin, J. (1989). Women's changing work roles: Impact on health, family and public policy. *American Psychologist, 44,* 1389–1393. Copyright 1989 by the American Psychological Association. Reprinted by permission.

QUESTIONS FOR EXERCISE 4

1. The authors state that "As Figure 1 shows, rates have increased throughout the century." In your opinion, does Figure 1 support this statement? Explain.

2. Compare Figure 1 with the first paragraph in the excerpt. If you were the author of this article, would you have included only the paragraph, only the figure, or both the paragraph and the figure? Explain.

3. The increase from 1986 to 1987 is smaller than the increase from 1970 to 1980. Speculate on the possible reason(s) for this.

4. Note that this article was published in 1989. To provide a dot for 1990, the authors would have had to use a projection. Instead, the authors chose to use actual data for 1986 and 1987. Do you think that this was a good decision? Explain.

5. How does the second paragraph in the excerpt affect your interpretation of Figure 1? Explain.

6. For which subgroup of women was there a decrease in the percentage employed from 1975 to 1986?

7. The increase for divorced women from 1975 to 1986 was only about four percent. Speculate on why this is so much lower than the increase for all women, which is about ten percent.

8. Notice that the drawing is called a "figure" rather than a "table." (See exercises 1 through 3 for examples of tables.) What is the difference between a "statistical figure" and a "statistical table"?

9. Keeping in mind that the titles (i.e., captions) of figures should be brief, comment on the adequacy of the title given to Figure 1.

10. Note that in the excerpt the figure number and title (i.e., caption) are placed *above* the figure. If you have a statistics or research methods textbook, check to see whether the textbook authors also place the numbers and titles of figures above their figures. Write your findings here.

11. Do your textbook authors also place the numbers and titles (i.e., captions) of tables *above their tables* as was done in the excerpts in exercises 1 through 3?

12. What information in the excerpt do you find the most interesting or surprising? Explain.

Notes:

EXERCISE 5

BEHAVIOR OF TWO MAINSTREAMED STUDENTS

STATISTICAL GUIDE

In an experiment, researchers manipulate the subjects' environment and measure the responses of the subjects. In some experiments, there are baseline periods in which there is no special manipulation; hence these periods are control periods, which are used as a standard for evaluating the effects of the manipulation.

Interobserver reliability indicates the extent to which two or more observers who have made independent observations agree with each other.

BACKGROUND NOTES

A mainstreamed student is one with special needs who is placed in a regular classroom.

In this study, subject A was classified as emotionally disturbed and subject B was classified as learning disabled. During the intervention periods, students earned tokens for on-task behaviors (e.g., eyes on the teacher when appropriate) that could be exchanged for rewards. In the figures shown below, the data for Baseline I were obtained before the introduction of tokens; during Baseline II, the tokens were withdrawn.

In the following excerpt, the authors use the term "significant increase" in its everyday sense, meaning an increase of practical importance or consequence.

EXCERPT FROM THE RESEARCH ARTICLE

A trained independent observer recorded the subjects' on-task behavior during language arts using a partial-interval recording system of 10-second intervals. Reliability was calculated by dividing the number of agreements by the number of agreements and disagreements for each observation and multiplying by 100.

For subject A, interobserver reliability measures were taken on 38% of the sessions and across all phases.

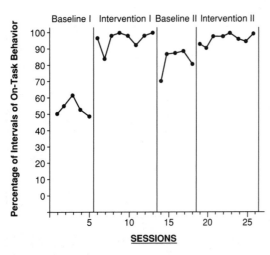

Fig. 1. Percentage of intervals of on-task behavior for Subject A.

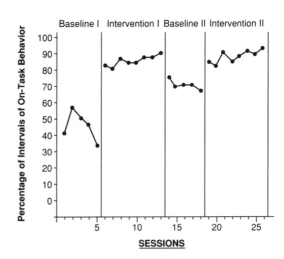

Fig. 2. Percentage of intervals of on-task behavior for Subject B.

Reliability measures ranged from 92% to 100%. Interobserver reliability measures for subject B were taken on 35% of the sessions and across all phases. Reliability ranged from 92% to 100%.

The results are presented in Figures 1 and 2. The intervention resulted in a significant increase in both subjects' on-task behavior.

SOURCE: Salend, S. J., Tintle, L., & Balber, H. (1988). Effects of a student-managed response-cost system on the behavior of two mainstreamed students. *The Elementary School Journal, 89,* 89–97. Copyright 1988 by The University of Chicago Press. Reprinted with permission.

QUESTIONS FOR EXERCISE 5

1. Do you agree with the assertion in the last sentence of the excerpt? Explain.

2. Do you believe that an initial five-day baseline period is sufficient in a study of this type? Explain.

3. Note that in the excerpt the figure numbers and titles (i.e., captions) are placed *below* the figures. If you have a statistics or research methods textbook, check to see whether the textbook authors also place the numbers and titles of figures below their figures. Write your findings here.

4. Speculate on why the observer recorded at 10-second intervals instead of recording each and every behavior of the subjects.

5. Speculate on why interobserver reliability measures were taken on only 35 to 38 percent of the sessions.

6. Suppose you conducted a similar study and for one observation session, the two observers agreed 29 times and disagreed 3 times. Using the procedures for calculating interobserver agreement described in the excerpt, what reliability, expressed as a percentage, should you report?

7. For both subjects, there was a higher percentage of on-task behaviors during Baseline II than during Baseline I. Does this seem reasonable? Explain.

8. Would the results in Figure 1 have appeared to be more or less dramatic if the authors had deleted the lower portion of the figure (i.e., from 40 percent down on the vertical or y axis)? Before answering this question, cover the lower portion of the figure with your hand or a piece of paper. Explain.

9. What information in the excerpt do you find the most interesting or surprising? Explain.

Notes:

EXERCISE 6

YOUNG CHILDREN WHO DROWN IN HOT TUBS

STATISTICAL GUIDE

A histogram has vertical bars. The scores on a continuous variable are placed on the horizontal axis (i.e., *x*-axis). For example, "age" is a continuous variable because there are no gaps between ages zero and one, between one and two, etc. The vertical axis (i.e, *y*-axis) shows the frequency or rate of occurrence.

An outlier is an observation that is far from the other observations. For example, Figure 2 contains some outliers.

EXCERPT FROM THE RESEARCH ARTICLE

Data for this study were obtained from the California Master Mortality File which contains information from the death certificate.

Between 1960 and 1979, there were only 15 drowning cases, but with the increasing popularity of residential hot tubs, spas and whirlpools (Monroe, 1982), 59 cases were reported from 1980 to 1985. The annual rates per million children aged 0-14 are shown in Figure 1. The actual number of hot tubs, spas, or whirlpools in California is unknown but is increasing according to sales figures.

Children who drowned ranged in age from 10 to 41 months in 90 percent of the cases and from 3-1/2 to 11 years in the remaining 10 percent (Figure 2). Fifty-two of the 74 cases (70 percent) were ages 10 to 23 months; and in this age group, the male:female ratio was 1.2:1. All 11 children over 3 years of age who drowned were males; and the three cases of entrapment by suction occurred in males aged 9 or 10 years.

SOURCE: Shinaberger, C. S., Anderson, C. L., & Kraus, J. F. (1990). Young children who drown in hot tubs, spas, and whirlpools in California: A 26-year survey. *American Journal of Public Health, 80*, 613–614. Copyright 1990 by the American Public Health Association. Reprinted by permission.

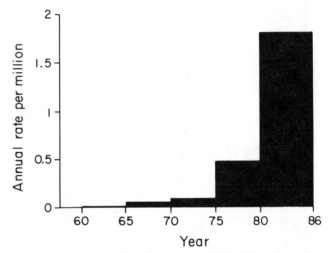

FIGURE 1—Annual Rate of Hot Tub, Spa, or Whirlpool Drownings among Children Ages 0–14 Years, California, 1960–85

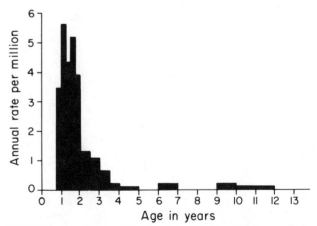

FIGURE 2—Annual Rate of Hot Tub, Spa or Whirlpool Drownings, by A among Children Ages 0–14 Years, California, 1960–85

21

QUESTIONS FOR EXERCISE 6

1. During which period shown in Figure 1 was the rate of drowning the highest?

2. What was the rate of drowning for children who were eight years old?

3. The authors mention the male-to-female ratio. According to this ratio, was the rate higher for males or for females?

4. Why do you think the authors chose to report the *rate per million* (i.e., the number of cases per million) in the figures instead of the raw frequencies (i.e., number of cases) per year?

5. Much of the information in Figure 2 is also described by the authors in the excerpt. Do you believe that Figure 2 is an important part of this report? Explain.

6. Note that the authors have labeled their histograms as "figures"—not as "tables." Is this appropriate? Explain.

7. In the text, the authors refer to 1960 to 1985; Figure 1 shows 1960 to 1986. Speculate on the reason for this apparent discrepancy.

8. The authors used five-year periods in Figure 1. Comment on other choices that the authors might have made such as presenting one bar for each year or one bar for each decade.

9. Overall, do the histograms suggest to you striking trends? Explain.

10. Briefly describe the outliers in Figure 2.

11. In the article, the authors conclude, among other things, that "residential hot tubs, spas or whirlpools represent a . . . high-risk drowning site for young children." Based on the excerpt, do you agree with this conclusion? Explain.

12. Note that in the excerpt the figure numbers and titles (i.e., captions) are placed *below* the figures. If you have a statistics or research methods textbook, check to see whether the textbook authors also place the numbers and titles of figures below their figures. Write your findings here.

Notes:

EXERCISE 7

HAND MANIPULATION SKILLS

STATISTICAL GUIDE

A frequency polygon indicates the frequency or number of subjects at various score levels. In the polygon shown below, the scores are grouped (e.g., scores from 20 through 29 are in one group and the number of children in that grouping of scores is shown).

A normal distribution has a smooth, symmetrical bell shape when plotted as a frequency polygon.

BACKGROUND NOTES

The following excerpt is drawn from a report on a study in which children were first tested without being given cues on how to perform the tasks. Two to seven days later, they were retested, but this time each child was given either a verbal or visual cue for each item on the test.

EXCERPT FROM THE RESEARCH ARTICLE

Twenty-eight children participated in the study.

Five sets of materials were presented in this study: (a) nickels and a bank, (b) small pegs and a pegboard, (c) markers and paper, (d) clay (to form into a ball), and (e) small erasers that fit into plastic containers with lids. These materials were selected to elicit the following in-hand manipulation skills: (a) finger-to-palm and palm-to-finger translation . . . , (b) shift . . . , and (c) rotation. The items were scored according to whether a particular in-hand manipulation was present or absent. The maximum total in-hand manipulation score possible was 78.

In the uncued (pretest) version, each child was told the end product for the task, but not the process to use in accomplishing the task, for example, "Put the money in the bank, one at a time."

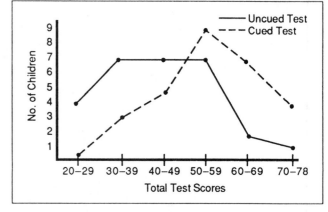

Figure 1. Total scores of the children for the uncued (pretest) and cued (posttest) versions of the In-Hand Manipulation Test.

The instructions used in the uncued version of the test were also used in the cued (posttest) version. The verbal and visual cues were provided. . . . For the visual cues, I said "Watch how I do this and see if you can do it like I did it." For the verbal cues, I emphasized to the children that they should move the materials with their fingers and not use their other hand or their body to help move the object.

Figure 1 illustrates the pattern of scores for the cued and uncued tests. A normal distribution of scores was expected for both sets of data.

Cuing appeared to produce a significant increase in the overall scores of the 3- and 4-year-old children.

Some increase in scores might have occurred regardless of cuing; I did not assess this possibility because a control group could not be included in the study.

SOURCE: Exner, C. E. (1990). The zone of proximal development in in-hand manipulation skills of nondysfunctional 3- and 4-year-old children. *The American Journal of Occupational Therapy, 44,* 884–891. Copyright 1990 by the American Occupational Therapy Association, Inc. Reprinted with permission.

QUESTIONS FOR EXERCISE 7

1. When the uncued test was administered, how many children scored in the top interval (i.e., 70–78)?

2. When the cued test was administered, how many children scored in the top interval (i.e., 70–78)?

3. Are your answers to questions 1 and 2 consistent with the author's interpretation that cuing appeared to produce an increase in scores? Explain.

4. Speculate on why the highest class interval (i.e., 70–78) is smaller than the other intervals.

5. What is your opinion on the use of an interval size of ten for grouping the scores? (Note: Scores from 20 through 29 cover ten points; the highest interval covers nine points.)

6. Has the decision to group data caused a loss of information? Explain.

7. Do you believe that there are disadvantages to using ungrouped data on the horizontal axis? That is, are there disadvantages to listing each score from 20 to 78 and plotting the frequency for each? Explain.

8. The authors of some textbooks recommend that each polygon should begin and end with a frequency of zero. This is accomplished by including one interval below the lowest score and one interval above the highest score. At these intervals, of course, the frequencies are zero. The author who produced Figure 1 above did not do this. In your opinion, has information been lost as a result of not following this recommendation? Explain.

9. The author begins the frequency polygon with the interval 20–29 instead of 0–9 because the lowest scoring subject scored between 20 and 29. Has the decision not to show data below 20 caused a loss of information? Explain.

10. Do either of the curves appear to represent a normal distribution? Explain.

11. Do you believe that the use of a control group in a follow-up study on this topic would be desirable? Explain.

12. In your opinion, is it desirable to give each figure a number (e.g., "Figure 1")? Why?

Notes:

EXERCISE 8

SPELLING COMPONENT TEST

STATISTICAL GUIDE

A cumulative percentage indicates the percentage of subjects who scored at and below a given score level. When rounded to a whole number, a cumulative percentage can be thought of as a percentile rank. For example, if 40 percent of a norm group scored at or below an examinee's score, then that examinee has a percentile rank of 40.

EXCERPT FROM THE RESEARCH ARTICLE

This test is composed of 76 words with one or more letters missing. A short line indicates where the letter(s) should be inserted (e.g., exper____ment). Words were selected from lists of the words most frequently misspelled by college students. Brief hints are provided in ambiguous or potentially difficult situations (e.g., capt____n/military rank). The test is timed at 10 minutes.

A sample of 316 undergraduate university students was tested on the Spelling Component Test. Results from this administration were combined with the 386 subjects tested in Study 1 to furnish a normative sample of 702 university students (407 females and 295 males).

The normative distribution of scores, for the full sample and separated by gender, is given in Table 3, in terms of cumulative percentages.

Table 3   Norms for the Spelling Component Test Based on 702 University Undergraduate Students

	Cumulative Percentage		
Score	Females (N = 407)	Males (N = 295)	Total (N = 702)
15-16	0.3	0.4	0.3
17-18	0.3	1.2	1.0
19-20	0.9	3.7	2.0
21-22	1.4	4.1	2.5
23-24	2.0	6.2	3.6
25-26	4.0	8.7	5.7
27-28	6.1	11.2	7.9
29-30	8.1	14.5	11.2
31-32	11.2	17.8	14.3
33-34	16.4	24.4	20.4
35-36	20.5	30.2	25.0
37-38	25.6	38.2	31.0
39-40	31.7	43.8	36.8
41-42	36.9	49.2	42.5
43-44	45.0	53.3	48.8
45-46	53.0	61.2	56.7
47-48	59.0	68.2	63.2
49-50	63.4	72.3	67.5
51-52	67.4	76.0	71.4
53-54	70.9	79.3	74.7
55-56	76.1	84.7	79.8
57-58	83.0	87.6	85.2
59-60	88.0	93.0	90.5
61-62	92.5	95.5	93.9
63-64	94.8	97.1	95.9
65-66	97.1	99.6	98.2
67-68	98.6	99.6	99.0
69-70	99.4	99.6	99.5

SOURCE: Coren, S. (1989). The Spelling Component Test: Psychometric evaluation and norms. *Educational and Psychological Measurement, 49*, 961–971. Copyright 1989 by Educational and Psychological Measurement. Reprinted by permission.

QUESTIONS FOR EXERCISE 8

1. What percentage of the females scored at and below scores of 47–48?

2. What percentage of the males scored at and below 47–48?

3. Based on a comparison of your answers to questions 1 and 2, did females or males apparently perform better on the test? Explain.

4. If the test were being used for college admissions, would a female who scored 47 be better off if her percentile rank was derived from the female norms or from the norms for the total sample? Explain.

5. If the test were being used for college admissions, would a male who scored 56 be better off if his percentile rank was derived from the male norms or from the norms for the total group? Explain.

6. The author grouped the raw scores into intervals of two points each (e.g., 15–16). Do you believe that the loss of information caused by the grouping is an important loss? Explain.

7. There were 76 items on the test. Yet, the highest score in the table is 70. Does this make sense? Explain.

8. Elsewhere in the report, the author states that 12 was the lowest score actually obtained. Yet, the table starts with a score of 15. Does the author's decision to start with 15 in the table seem reasonable? Explain.

9. The author of the table arranged the scores from lowest at the top to highest at the bottom. If you have a statistics book, determine whether your textbook author recommends the same arrangement and write your findings here.

10. Based on the norms for the total sample, what is the percentile rank for a subject who obtained a score of 38?

11. Based on the norms for the female sample, what is the percentile rank for a female subject who obtained a score of 38?

12. Based on the norms for the male sample, what is the percentile rank for a male subject who obtained a score of 38?

Notes:

EXERCISE 9

ENTREPRENEUR AND COLLEGE BUSINESS STUDENT VALUES

STATISTICAL GUIDE

When ranking, it is customary to give a rank of one (1) to the most important or desirable characteristic, a rank of two (2) to the next most important, etc. Thus, the lower the value of the rank, the more important or desirable the characteristic.

The median is defined as the average that indicates the value below which half of the subjects lie. For example, if the median for a group is 10.0, then 50 percent of the subjects lie below 10.0 and 50 percent lie above 10.0.

BACKGROUND NOTES

The subjects in the following study were entrepreneurs in Florida and senior-level undergraduate business students attending a university in Florida. The subjects ranked the 18 values listed in Table 3. The medians of the ranks for each value are shown for the female subjects.

EXCERPT FROM THE RESEARCH ARTICLE

For the sample of entrepreneurs, eighty-six (43 percent) of the males and eighty-two (41 percent) of the females returned the survey. Incomplete data was provided by both male and female respondents which decreased the useable responses to seventy-two (36 percent) and seventy-four (37 percent), respectively. The response from the student sample was much better with 79.8 percent completing the survey. The useable surveys amounted to 123, giving a response rate of 76.9 percent.

Table 3   Median Rankings for Female Entrepreneurs and Students

Value	Female Entrepreneurs $N = 74$	Female Students $N = 66$
A Comfortable Life	9.5	10.5
An Exciting Life	11.5	9.5
A Sense of Accomplishment	7.0	10.0
A World at Peace	11.0	10.0
A World of Beauty	13.0	10.0
Equality	13.0	8.5
Family Security	5.0	8.0
Freedom	5.0	9.0
Health	4.0	9.0
Inner Harmony	8.0	6.0
Mature Love	10.5	9.5
National Security	14.0	9.5
Pleasure	13.0	8.5
Salvation	17.0	10.0
Self-Respect	5.0	7.0
Social Recognition	14.0	11.0
True Friendship	8.5	12.0
Wisdom	8.0	13.0

Additional efforts are required before the findings herein reported can be considered meaningful. [Additional studies] comparing entrepreneur and business student values should be performed using larger national samples.

SOURCE: Solomon, G. T. & Fernald, L. W. (1990). A comparative analysis of entrepreneur and college business student values. *Journal of Creative Behavior, 24*, 238–255. Reprinted with permission of the copyright holder, Creative Education Foundation, Buffalo, New York.

QUESTIONS FOR EXERCISE 9

1. On the average, the female entrepreneurs ranked which value as the most important?

2. On the average, the female students ranked which value as the most important?

3. According to the medians, the female entrepreneurs ranked which value as the least important?

4. What percentage of the female students gave "inner harmony" a rank of 6.0 or less?

5. How many of the female students gave "inner harmony" a rank of 6.0 or less?

6. Comment on the authors' decision to report medians rather than means as the averages in this table. If you have a statistics textbook, first read the section on the appropriate uses of each average.

7. Assume that you are writing a term paper on the importance that female entrepreneurs and business students place on health. In a sentence, summarize the results shown in Table 3.

8. Speculate on what effect, if any, the failure of some subjects to respond might have had on the results.

9. Speculate on why the response rate for the students was higher than the response rate for the entrepreneurs.

10. In the last paragraph of the excerpt, the authors warn their readers that their results might not be meaningful. In your opinion, is such self-criticism appropriate in a scientific article?

11. What information in Table 3 is the most interesting or surprising? Explain.

Notes:

EXERCISE 10

NEW JERSEY'S INTENSIVE SUPERVISION PROGRAM

STATISTICAL GUIDE

To review the median, see the statistical guide for exercise 9.

The mean is the balance point in a distribution. It is calculated by summing all the scores and dividing by the number of scores. As a result, the mean is pulled toward extreme scores in an unbalanced distribution (i.e., a skewed distribution with extreme scores on one side without extreme scores on the other side to balance it out.) Because the median is insensitive to extreme scores, the mean and median do not always have the same value for a given distribution.

BACKGROUND NOTES

In the following excerpt, the comparison group (i.e., control group) is called the CLOSE OTI group. Their name comes from the fact that they were 130 individuals who had served ordinary terms of imprisonment (OTI) and were closely matched with the subjects who participated in the Intensive Supervision Program (ISP) in terms of criminal records and sociodemographic background variables. The CLOSE OTI group served sentences before implementation of the ISP program.

EXCERPT FROM THE RESEARCH ARTICLE

New Jersey's Intensive Supervision Program (ISP) has an active caseload of approximately 500 nonviolent offenders. ISP requires employment and provides a high frequency of field contacts with participants, including random tests to detect drug use. Because ISP requires that participants first serve a few months in prison, perform community service, and obey curfews, it provides a level of punishment intermediate between probation and ordinary terms of imprisonment.

The ISP group served a median of 109 days in prison, whereas the CLOSE OTI comparison group served a median of 308 days. Thus ISP saved about 200 prison days per participant.

The average cost per ISP offender for the typical correctional period (including 109 days in prison at $59, then 449 days in ISP at $15) is approximately $13,000. The average cost per [CLOSE] OTI offender for the offender's typical correctional period (308 days in prison at $50, then 896 days on parole at $2 to $3) is approximately $20,000 to $21,000. The estimated cost savings is approximately $7,000 per offender for the combined period of imprisonment and supervision in the community.

The Intensive Supervision Program requires that offenders be employed, and indeed it has produced a high rate of employment. . . . The participants' median yearly gross income while in ISP was approximately $10,000. The CLOSE OTI offenders' median yearly income while on parole (adjusted upward to take inflation into account) was roughly $5,000. The high employment levels resulted in an *increase* in legitimate earnings (compared to CLOSE OTI) of roughly $5,000 (using medians) or $4,000 (measured using means) per person per year.

ISP participants had lower recidivism rates than did offenders in the comparison groups. In most analyses, the new conviction rate of the ISP group averaged roughly 10 percentage points lower than that of the matched OTI group.

However, because random assignment to a true control group was not permitted by ISP policy makers, it is possible that some or all of the observed significant decrease in recidivism was due to the selective screening component of the Intensive Supervision Program, instead of (or in addition to) its supervision and counseling components.

SOURCE: Pearson, F. S. (1988). Evaluation of New Jersey's Intensive Supervision Program. *Crime & Delinquency, 34*, 437–448. Reprinted with permission.

QUESTIONS FOR EXERCISE 10

1. What percentage of the ISP group served more than 109 days in prison?

2. What percentage of the ISP group served less than 109 days in prison?

3. Fifty percent of the CLOSE OTI group served more than how many days in prison?

4. Does it surprise you that the average ISP participant spent less time in prison than the average individual in the CLOSE OTI? Explain.

5. Speculate on which average is reported in the first sentence of the third paragraph of the excerpt.

6. The author could have reported the total cost for those in each group and reported this information in the third paragraph. Instead, he chose to calculate and report averages. Why was this decision appropriate?

7. The author reports approximate averages in the third paragraph. Do you think that the use of approximations is appropriate? Explain.

8. Approximately what percentage of the ISP participants earned more than $10,000 per year?

9. Is the difference in average gross annual incomes greater when measured with means or when measured with medians?

10. Does the difference referred to in question 9 surprise you? Explain.

11. Suppose that several members of the CLOSE OTI group earned substantially more than most of the others in their group. What effect would this have on the mean gross annual income of this group?

12. The author suggests that random assignment to form a control group would have been a better procedure (i.e., better than using a previous group of prisoners matched on background variables). Do you agree? Explain.

13. What information in the excerpt do you find the most interesting or surprising? Explain.

Notes:

EXERCISE 11

MASS-MEDIA ADVERTISING CLAIMS

STATISTICAL GUIDE

To review the median, see the guide for exercise 9; to review the mean, see the guide for exercise 10.

The range indicates the number of score points—from lowest to highest—covered by a distribution of scores. The interquartile range indicates the points covered by the middle 50 percent of the subjects. Put another way, if all the scores are put in order from low to high and the bottom 25 percent and top 25 percent are ignored, the range of the remaining scores is the interquartile range.

EXCERPT FROM THE RESEARCH ARTICLE

The print study involved testing 108 test communications (54 ads and 54 editorial excerpts) using a sample of 1347 individuals which were broadly representative of magazine readers across the U.S. Each respondent read and responded to four test communications (two ads and two editorials). Benefitting from the criticisms of the earlier TV study, the print investigation included an explicit "don't know" response option in order to lower respondents' propensity to guess. . . . [Comprehension] was measured via a set of six true-false statements designed to tap into the universe of explicit [i.e., factual] and implicit [i.e., inferential] meanings that could be conveyed by each of the test communications.

Results of the item-level analysis for the comprehension measures are presented in Table 3. At an overall level, the median level of accurate comprehension was 68.0 percent (63.2 percent mean) with the rate of comprehension being higher for advertising than for editorial content (70.0 percent versus 65.3 percent; 65.4 percent versus 60.8 percent mean). The range of scores spanned the entire spectrum of possibilities (0 percent to 100 percent).

It can be seen from Table 3 that the overall interquartile range is 47.1 percent to 82.4 percent. The interquartile range for the 54 advertisements was 52.0 percent to 84.0 percent. Thus, under typical circumstances, we might expect readers to comprehend anywhere from half to over three quarters of the print meanings to which they are exposed.

Table 3   Individual Item Analysis—Comprehension—Print Study

	Median	Range (%)	Interquartile Range (%)
Overall	68.0	0 to 100	47.1 to 82.4
ADS	70.0	6.0 to 100	52.0 to 84.0
Facts	70.0	18.0 to 100	54.0 to 82.4
Inferences	72.0	6.0 to 80.4	46.0 to 88.0
EDS	65.3	0 to 100	44.0 to 80.4
Facts	65.3	0 to 100	47.1 to 80.0
Inferences	64.7	8.0 to 96.1	38.8 to 82.0

SOURCE: Jacoby, J. & Hoyer, W. D. (1990). The misconception of mass-media advertising claims: A re-analysis of benchmark data. *Journal of Advertising Research, 30,* 9–16. Copyright 1990 by the Advertising Research Council. Reprinted with permission.

QUESTIONS FOR EXERCISE 11

1. Which of the statistics in Table 3 is a measure of central tendency (i.e., an average)?

   A. Median.   B. Range.   C. Interquartile range.

2. Do the means or medians suggest a higher rate of comprehension?

3. Overall, what percentage of the subjects marked less than 68 percent of the items correctly?

4. Overall, what percentage of the subjects marked less than 47.1 percent of the items correctly?

5. Overall, what percentage of the subjects marked more than 82.4 percent of the items correctly?

6. For which type of item was the range the smallest? (Circle one.)

   A. ADS–Facts   B. ADS–Inferences   C. EDS–Facts   D. EDS–Inferences

7. All of the interquartile ranges are smaller than the ranges. Does this make sense? Explain.

8. In general, was the rate of comprehension for the ads or for the editorials higher? Explain.

9. If you have a statistics text, look up the definition of the range. Did the authors of the excerpt compute the range in the way that the author of your text suggests? Explain.

10. If you have a statistics text, look up the range and interquartile range. Does the author of your textbook prefer one over the other? Explain.

11. In your opinion, do the results suggest that advertisements are clear in meaning to most consumers? Explain.

12. What information in the excerpt do you find the most interesting or surprising? Explain.

Notes:

EXERCISE 12

ADOLESCENT DRUG ABUSERS

STATISTICAL GUIDE

The standard deviation is a yardstick for measuring variability (i.e., differences among subjects). Synonyms for "variability" are "spread" and "dispersion." The larger the value of the standard deviation, the greater the variability.

In a normal distribution (i.e., a type of symmetrical, bell-shaped distribution), about 34 percent of the subjects lie within one standard deviation unit on each side of the mean. For example, if $SD = 10.00$ for a normal distribution, then one standard deviation unit equals 10 points, and 68 percent of the subjects lie within (i.e., plus and minus) 10 points of the mean (34 percent on each side of the mean).

BACKGROUND NOTE

The subjects in this study were all drug abusers attending outpatient treatment programs. The following excerpt was provided as background information on the 169 subjects prior to treatment.

EXCERPT FROM THE RESEARCH ARTICLE

The client study sample was predominately male, white and Catholic. . . . The age range was 14–21, with a mean age of 17.9 years ($SD = 1.84$). The mean number of years of education completed (9.3 years; $SD = 1.44$) is significantly below the norm for a sample that has a mean age of 17.9 years.

Table 3   Substance Use of Client Subject Sample

Drug	Used Past Year %	Used Past 3 Months %	# Times Used Past Month		Age at First Use	
			M	SD	M	SD
Alcohol	95	88	8.6	14.1	12.7	1.9
Marijuana	94	87	25.7	31.6	12.6	2.3
Inhalants	8	7	0.8	4.6	14.1	2.2
Amphetamines	69	52	7.1	20.7	14.6	1.5
Barbiturates	20	15	1.1	5.9	14.3	1.7
Tranquilizers	36	23	1.0	4.5	14.8	1.3
Sedatives	24	14	0.9	4.7	14.7	1.5
PCP	30	15	0.7	3.4	15.0	1.4
Hallucinogens	34	22	0.8	4.0	14.5	1.4
Cocaine	41	28	1.4	7.7	15.4	1.5
Heroin	5	5	0.7	4.0	15.0	1.1
Other opiates	18	11	0.4	2.3	14.9	1.9
Other drugs	3	2	0.2	2.3	13.5	2.4
Nonprescription	10	6	0.1	1.0	14.9	1.5

SOURCE: Friedman, A. S. (1989). Family therapy vs. parent groups: Effects on adolescent drug abusers. *The American Journal of Family Therapy, 17*, 335–347. Copyright 1989 by Brunner/Mazel, Inc. Reprinted by permission.

QUESTIONS FOR EXERCISE 12

1. Of the 169 subjects, how many reported using marijuana during the past year?

2. How many of the subjects reported using inhalants during the past three months?

3. Almost all of the percentages in the "used past year" column are higher than the percentages in the "used past 3 months" column. Does this seem reasonable? Explain.

4. On the average, how many times was cocaine used in the past month?

5. Which column in the table provides the most useful information if one wants to know which drug was most frequently used by the subjects?

6. On the average, which drug was first used at the earliest age?

7. For which drug is there the greatest variability in terms of number of times used in the past month?

8. Which drug category had the least spread in terms of number of times used in the past month?

9. Which drug category had the greatest dispersion in terms of age at first use?

10. Assuming that the distribution of age at first use for PCP is normal, what percentage of the subjects first used PCP between the ages of 13.6 and 16.4?

11. Assuming that the distribution of age at first use of heroin is normal, what percentage of the subjects first used heroin between the ages of 15.0 and 16.1?

12. Assuming that the distribution of age at first use of alcohol is normal, what percentage of the subjects first used alcohol between the ages of 10.8 and 12.7?

13. Do you believe that the mean for age at first use of heroin is probably based on all 169 subjects or on only a subgroup of the 169 subjects? Explain.

Notes:

EXERCISE 13

MENTORING AMONG MEN AND WOMEN

STATISTICAL GUIDE

Note that the symbol for the mean in the excerpt is *M*.

Some of the variables in this report are dichotomous (i.e., have only two categories each such as "single" or "married"). These are treated here as quantitative data by assigning a number to each category.

If you go out about two standard deviation units on both sides of the mean in a normal distribution, you capture approximately 95 percent of the cases. (The precise rule for capturing 95 percent of the cases is given in the next exercise.) If you go out three standard deviation units on both sides of the mean, you capture 99.7 percent of the cases.

EXCERPT FROM THE RESEARCH ARTICLE

The data for this field study were collected with a mail survey of business-school graduates from two large state universities in the United States. We used alumni records to obtain the addresses of graduates from bachelor's and master's degree programs. A survey questionnaire was sent to a stratified random sample of 1,000 business school graduates.

Table 2   Means and Standard Deviations for Analysis Variables for Men and Women

Variable	Women (*n* = 147)		Men (*n* = 173)	
	M	SD	M	SD
Degree (bachelor's = 0, master's = 1)	0.52	0.50	0.64	0.48
Previous experience (years)	2.29	3.39	2.24	3.54
Years since graduation	7.37	2.59	7.96	2.66
Employment interruptions (months)	2.75	5.67	1.80	4.11
Organization size[a]	5.09	2.34	5.16	2.31
Industry (service = 0, manufacturing = 1)	0.17	0.38	0.28	0.45
Socioeconomic status[b]	4.13	0.95	4.10	0.81
Marital status (single = 0, married = 1)	0.60	0.49	0.73	0.44
Promotions	3.32	1.82	3.52	2.24
Total income ($)	45,335.67	21,719.87	57,563.08	33,887.65
Pay-level satisfaction	3.43	0.94	3.39	0.92
Benefits satisfaction	3.69	0.99	3.70	0.92

[a]Coded as follows: 1-50 employees (1); 50-99 employees (2); 100-499 employees (3); 500-999 employees (4); 1,000-4,999 employees (5); 5,000-9,999 employees (6); 10,000-49,999 employees (7); and 50,000 or more employees (8). [b]Coded as underclass (1); working poor (2); working class (3); middle class (4); upper middle class (5); and upper class (6).

SOURCE: Dreher, G. F. & Ash, R. A. (1990). A comparative study of mentoring among men and women in managerial, professional, and technical positions. *Journal of Applied Psychology, 75,* 539–546. Copyright 1990 by the American Psychological Association. Reprinted by permission.

QUESTIONS FOR EXERCISE 13

1. On the average, by how many dollars did the income for men exceed the income for women?

2. Were the incomes for men or the incomes for women more variable?

3. Was there more spread in months of employment interruptions for men or for women?

4. After rounding the mean for organization size for women to a whole number, you should conclude that the average woman worked in an organization with about how many employees?

5. Was the average socioeconomic status for men closer to "middle class" or closer to "upper middle class?"

6. On the average, were more men or more women married?

7. Assuming that the distribution of benefits satisfaction for women is normal, about what percentage of women had scores between 1.71 and 5.67?

8. Assuming that the distribution of pay-level satisfaction for men is normal, what percentage of men had scores between 0.63 and 6.15?

9. Assuming that the distribution of years since graduation for men is normal, between what two values did approximately the middle 95 percent of the men lie?

10. Assuming that the distribution of socioeconomic status for women is normal, between what two values did the middle 99.7 percent of the women lie?

11. The variable "degree" is dichotomous. The authors chose to describe the results for this variable using means and standard deviations. What other statistics could have been used to describe the subjects' standing on this variable?

12. The standard deviations for the dichotomous variables are small (i.e., all are less than 1.0). Do such small standard deviations make sense? Explain.

Notes:

EXERCISE 14

IRRATIONAL BELIEFS AND THREE INTERPERSONAL STYLES

STATISTICAL GUIDE

If you go out 1.96 standard deviation units on both sides of the mean, you capture 95 percent of the cases. (In the previous exercise, the approximate 95 percent rule was given.)

If you go out 2.58 standard deviation units on both sides of the mean, you capture 99 percent of the cases. (In the previous exercise, the 99.7 percent rule was given.)

EXCERPT FROM THE RESEARCH ARTICLE

The subjects were 217 undergraduate students enrolled in introductory psychology and general education courses at a community college in California. All subjects volunteered to participate in the study during regularly scheduled daytime classes. The subject sample consisted of 97 men and 120 women with a mean age of 21.1 yr. (SD = 1.7).

Irrational beliefs were measured by the Irrational Beliefs Test (Jones, 1968), a measure of 10 commonly held irrational beliefs identified by Ellis (1962). The test consists of 100 item-statements which measure the presence or absence of a particular irrational belief (10 items per belief). For each statement subjects rate themselves according to five choices ranging from strongly agree to strongly disagree. A maximum raw score possible on any scale is 50, and a minimum score is 10. Table 1 lists subjects' means and standard deviations.

Table 1   Summary of Irrational Beliefs

Irrational Beliefs	M	SD
1. Love and approval by significant others is a dire necessity.	30.93	5.13
2. One must be thoroughly competent to consider oneself worthwhile.	30.26	4.32
3. Some people are evil and must be judged and punished severely.	29.63	5.37
4. It is catastrophic when things do not work out as desired.	30.72	5.19
5. Unhappiness is externally caused and people can do little to control this.	25.03	5.42
6. One should dwell upon fearsome and dangerous possibilities.	28.76	6.89
7. It is easier to avoid than face certain difficulties.	25.28	5.14
8. One should be dependent upon others who are stronger.	27.61	4.56
9. We are virtually unable to overcome significant past influences.	25.20	5.35
10. There is a precise, perfect solution to human problems.	27.72	6.08

SOURCE: Reproduced with permission of author and publisher from Goldberg, G. M. (1990). Irrational beliefs and three interpersonal styles. *Psychological Reports, 66,* 963–969.

QUESTIONS FOR EXERCISE 14

1. On the average, which irrational belief was least strongly held by the subjects? Explain.

2. For which belief was there the greatest variability? Explain.

3. Which of the two statistics in Table 1 is a measure of central tendency?

4. The author did not arrange the beliefs in Table 1 in alphabetical order. Do you believe that he should have done so? Explain.

5. Speculate on why the minimum score is 10 and not 0.

6. Does the author state that the scores for his subjects actually ranged from 10 to 50? Explain.

7. Assuming that the distribution is normal, between what two scores does the middle 95 percent of the subjects lie on the first irrational belief? (Use the rule given above in the statistical guide.)

8. Assuming that the distribution is normal, between what two scores does the middle 99 percent of the subjects lie on the first irrational belief?

9. Compare your answers to questions 7 and 8. If your answers are correct, your answer to question 8 gives a larger range of values than your answer to question 7 does. Does this seem reasonable to you? Explain.

10. In exercises 10 through 12, you were asked to assume that the distributions are normal. Consult your statistics book to find out if the rules that you have been applying (such as using a multiplier of 1.96 to capture 95 percent of a distribution) apply if a distribution is clearly *not* normal. Write your findings here.

11. Assuming that the distribution is normal, what percentage of the cases lies above a score of 43.41 on the tenth belief?

12. What information in the excerpt do you find the most interesting or surprising? Explain.

Notes:

EXERCISE 15

THE STANFORD-BINET FOURTH EDITION

STATISTICAL GUIDE

Most standard scores, when expressed as z scores, range from -3.0 to +3.0, with a mean of 0 and a standard deviation of 1. (Note: A small fraction of 1 percent of z scores may be beyond the range stated above.) For a group of subjects, z scores can be computed by subtracting the group's mean from each score and dividing this difference by the standard deviation. Thus, z scores indicate how many standard deviation units each subject is from the mean.

Test makers often transform z scores to another scale with a new mean (usually a multiple of 10 that is above 0) and a new standard deviation. This is accomplished by multiplying each z score by the desired new standard deviation and adding to it the desired new mean.

BACKGROUND NOTE

The Stanford-Binet Fourth Edition (Binet 4) is an individually administered intelligence test. The z scores of the norm group have been transformed to the scales described below.

The excerpt provides background information on the Stanford-Binet.

EXCERPT FROM THE RESEARCH ARTICLE

The sample consisted of 5,013 subjects grouped at one year intervals from 1 to 17 years and an 18–through 23-year interval. The sample was stratified on age, sex, ethnic group, geographic region, and community size in accordance with data from the 1980 U.S. Census (Thorndike, Hagen, and Sattler, 1986, pp. 16–18). Shortcomings in the sampling procedure were corrected by weighting cases in accordance with U.S. Census statistics.

The Binet 4 consists of 15 subtests providing a Composite Standard Age Score. The Composite is divided into four content areas: (a) Verbal Reasoning, (b) Abstract/Visual Reasoning, (c) Quantitative Reasoning, and (d) Short Term Memory. All 15 subtests are not administered at every age level. Between 8 and 13 of the subtests are administered depending upon the subject's age and performance on the initial routing subtest, Vocabulary.

Each content area has a mean SAS of 100 and a standard deviation of 16, while each subtest standard score has a mean of 50 and a standard deviation of 8. Further information concerning test development and psychometric data can be found in the technical manual (Thorndike, et al., 1986).

SOURCE: Glaub, V. E. & Kamphaus, R. W. (1991). Construction of a nonverbal adaptation of the Stanford-Binet Fourth Edition. *Educational and Psychological Measurement, 51,* 231–241. Copyright 1991 by Educational and Psychological Measurement. Reprinted by permission.

QUESTIONS FOR EXERCISE 15

1. Suppose someone obtained a SAS of 50 on one of the individual subtests. Would you classify this person as above average, average, or below average? Explain.

2. Suppose someone obtained a SAS of 50 on one of the content area tests. Would you classify this person as above average, average, or below average? Explain.

3. If a person scores 116 on a contest area test, how many standard deviation units is the person above the mean? Explain.

4. If a person scores 42 on a subtest, how many standard deviation units is the person below the mean? Explain.

5. Given the range of standard scores described in the first sentence of the statistical guide, what is the highest SAS one might get on a content area test?

6. Given the range of standard scores described in the first sentence of the statistical guide, what is the lowest standard score on a subtest that one might get?

7. A person who gets a score of 50 on a subtest has what corresponding z score?

8. What is the value of the z score that corresponds to a SAS content area score of 132?

9. A person who earns a *z* score of -2 on Short Term Memory has what SAS on this section?

10. Suppose an examiner wants to compare an examinee's scores in the four content areas. Should the examiner use raw scores (i.e., number right) or the standard scores? Explain.

11. The authors of the test used a different transformation for the content areas than for the subtests. Does this seem like a good idea to you? Explain.

Notes:

EXERCISE 16

STATISTICS IN *PERCEPTION & PSYCHOPHYSICS*

STATISTICAL GUIDE

A scattergram (also known as a scatter diagram or scatter plot) depicts the relationship between two variables. For each case or subject, one dot is placed to show where the case stands on *both* variables.

In the excerpt, the author refers to significance tests. These are mathematical tests that help us decide whether a relationship or difference should be considered to be statistically significant in light of chance or random errors that may have affected the data. Significance tests are examined more closely later in this book.

EXCERPT FROM THE RESEARCH ARTICLE

I computed the percentage of articles in each volume [of *Perception & Psychophysics*] that reported at least one significance test. I then reread Volumes 1–10 as a reliability check, computing the percentage of articles reporting tests in the second reading. I computed the differences between percentages based on the first and second readings. Of those 10 differences, 1 was 8%, 8 were 3% or less, and 1 was 0.

The percentage of articles reporting significance tests in each volume is shown in Figure 1. The abscissa is year of publication; each data point represents a volume. Notice that there was only one volume in each of 1966 and 1967 and that there have been two volumes per year since then. For the data of Volumes 1–10 (the ones I recounted), the higher of my two counts is shown. Notice that the percentage of articles containing significance tests appears to increase over time, being around 65 to 70 in the first few volumes and around 85 recently. From 1966 to June 1978 (Volumes 1–23), in only five volumes did the percentage with tests reach 80, whereas the percentage exceeded 80 in all but five of Volumes 24–46.

There has been, over the years, a pronounced increase in the proportion of articles in the Psychonomic Society journal *Perception & Psychophysics* that use statistical significance tests in data analysis.

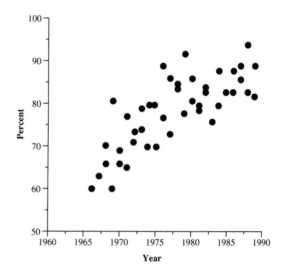

Fig. 1. Percentage of articles reporting the performing of statistical tests in each volume (one volume in 1966 and 1967; two volumes per year thereafter) by year.

SOURCE: Parker, S. (1990). A note on the growth of the use of statistical tests in *Perception & Psychophysics. Bulletin of the Psychonomic Society, 28*, 565–566. Copyright 1990. Reprinted by permission of the Psychonomic Society, Inc.

QUESTIONS FOR EXERCISE 16

1. Do you believe that the data on the percentage of articles containing significance tests are sufficiently reliable? Explain.

2. What name does the author use to refer to the horizontal axis (i.e., what is the formal name of the horizontal axis)?

3. If you have a statistics textbook, look up the formal name of the vertical axis and write it here.

4. Does Figure 1 contain one data point for each year or for each volume?

5. Is the relationship in Figure 1 direct (with one variable increasing while the other is increasing) or inverse (with one variable increasing while the other is decreasing)?

6. In 1966, about what percentage of the articles reported significance tests?

7. For the two most recent volumes, about what percentage of the articles reported significance tests?

8. Does Figure 1 add to your understanding of the author's interpretation that begins in the second paragraph with the words "Notice that the percentage of articles . . ."? Explain.

9. If you were asked to represent the dots with a single line, would you use a straight line or a curved line? Explain.

10. Do you agree that the relationship is "pronounced"? Explain.

11. If you have a statistics textbook, compare Figure 1 with scattergrams shown in your text. If there is a scattergram with a pattern similar to that in Figure 1, identify it by page number and figure number and describe how your textbook author characterizes the relationship.

12. After you have studied the next two exercises, decide whether the authors of those articles should have also included scattergrams. Write your decision with an explanation here.

Notes:

EXERCISE 17

APTITUDE TEST SCORES

STATISTICAL GUIDE

When a correlation coefficient (r) is positive, it indicates that those who score high on one variable tend to score high on the other. The strength of this tendency is indicated by the value of r. The closer it is to 1.00, the stronger the relationship; the closer it is to 0.00, the weaker it is. (Correlation coefficients may also be negative, which is illustrated in the next exercise.)

To obtain the variance on one variable "explained" by the other, square the r. For example, if $r = .50$, $r^2 = .25$, which is equivalent to 1/4 or 25 percent explained variance.

BACKGROUND NOTE

The Scholastic Aptitude Test (SAT) is a widely used test for admissions to undergraduate college programs; the Graduate Record Examination (GRE) is widely used for graduate school admissions.

EXCERPT FROM THE RESEARCH ARTICLE

The population of interest for the study consisted of examinees who took the SAT and also the GRE General Test at the normal times in their academic careers, with the typical number of years intervening.

Table 2   Intercorrelations Between SAT and GRE Scores for the Total Study Sample
$n = 22,923$

	SAT Verbal	SAT Mathematical	GRE Verbal	GRE Quantitative	GRE Analytical	Mean	Standard Deviation
SAT Verbal	1.000	.628	.858	.547	.637	518.8	104.7
SAT Mathematical	.628	1.000	.598	.862	.734	556.0	110.2
GRE Verbal	.858	.598	1.000	.560	.649	510.1	107.7
GRE Quantitative	.547	.862	.560	1.000	.730	573.4	125.6
GRE Analytical	.637	.734	.649	.730	1.000	579.7	117.6

Particularly interesting in Table 2 are the correlations between SAT-Verbal and GRE-Verbal and between SAT-Mathematical and GRE-Quantitative, both of which are .86, indicating that the linear relationship between SAT and GRE scores explains almost three fourths of the variance in GRE-Verbal and GRE-Quantitative scores taken 4 years later. These students were quite diverse in their academic interests, having gone their separate ways after high school into a wide variety of college majors, where their verbal and mathematical skills would be expected to undergo differential change. It is therefore particularly interesting that overall their rank order in these two general aptitude areas at the time of their junior or senior year in high school was so well preserved at the time of their application to graduate school.

SOURCE: Angoff, W. H. & Johnson, E. G. (1990). The differential impact of curriculum on aptitude test scores. *Journal of Educational Measurement, 27,* 291–305. Copyright 1990 by the National Council on Measurement in Education. Reprinted by permission of the publisher.

QUESTIONS FOR EXERCISE 17

1. Comment on the adequacy of the sample size.

2. The correlation between SAT-Verbal and SAT-Verbal is 1.00, which is perfect. Does this surprise you? Explain.

3. In words (not numbers) describe the direction and strength of the relationship between SAT-Verbal and GRE-Verbal.

4. To three decimal places, the relationship is strongest between which two variables? Explain. (Do not consider the Pearson r's with values of 1.000.)

5. The relationship between which two variables is weakest? Explain.

6. If you draw a diagonal line through all the r's that equal 1.00, you will find that the r's above the line are repeated below the line. Does this make sense? Explain.

7. Are the statistics in the last two columns of Table 2 measures of relationship? Explain.

8. How did the authors arrive at an explained variance of three fourths for a Pearson r of .86?

9. Expressed as a percentage, what is the explained variance between SAT-Verbal and GRE-Quantitative?

10. If your answer to question 9 is correct, it indicates that between one quarter and one third of the variance on a quantitative test is explained by the variance on a verbal test taken four years earlier. Does this surprise you? Explain.

11. In the excerpt, the authors refer to a "linear relationship." Look this term up in a statistics textbook and define it here.

12. In the last sentence of the excerpt, the authors refer to a "particularly interesting" finding. Do you agree that this finding would be of interest to educators and psychologists? Explain.

Notes:

EXERCISE 18

AIDS CONCERNS

STATISTICAL GUIDE

A positive value of *r* indicates that those who are high on one variable tend to be high on the other; also, those who are low on one tend to be low on the other. A negative value indicates that those who tend to be high on one variable tend to be low on the other.

The strength of these tendencies is indicated by the value of *r*. The closer *r* is to 1.00 or -1.00, the stronger the relationship.

EXCERPT FROM THE RESEARCH ARTICLE

The Michigan-Ontario Identification Association (MOIA) was founded in 1937 to represent the scientific interest of police crime scene investigators and evidence technicians. Although there are over 375 members throughout Ontario and Michigan, this research was limited only to those officers working in Michigan.

Questionnaires were sent to all 176 subjects on December 3, 1987. A second mailing went out to all subjects on January 12, 1988, with a cover letter instructing subjects to ignore the mailing if they had already responded. Completed questionnaires were returned by 132 subjects (75 percent); of these, all but 5 were usable. Conventional scientific thinking among survey researchers would consider this a high response rate, thus reducing the chances of any serious response bias.

[Within the questionnaire was] a 13-item scale labeled AIDS-WORRY, assessing the extent to which subjects indicate AIDS may be a source of stress or worry for themselves.

As shown in Table 2, subjects scoring high on the AIDS-WORRY scale tended to be younger, to rate their health better, to be of lower rank, to have less experience in law enforcement, and to report a greater frequency of contact "with blood, body fluids, or tissue when processing dead bodies, collecting blood samples, clothing, or evidence at a crime scene." Subjects were also asked whether their departmental guidelines "advise against eating, drinking, smoking, sticking anything in your mouth, wiping your mouth, nose, or eyes while in a crime scene where blood or body fluids are present." Subjects who disagreed with this guidelines statement scored much higher on the AIDS-WORRY scale.

Clear guidelines that incorporate the latest information on AIDS prevention should be developed and publicized.

Table 2   Correlates of AIDS-Worry Scale

Variable	n	r
Contact	118	+.24
Age	127	-.34
Health	125	+.21
Rank	116	-.19
Experience	127	-.26
Guidelines	127	-.41

SOURCE: Kennedy, D. B., Homant, R. J., & Emery, G. L. (1990). AIDS concerns among crime scene investigators. *Journal of Police Science and Administration, 17,* 12–19. Copyright 1990 by the International Association of Chiefs of Police, Inc. Reprinted with permission.

QUESTIONS FOR EXERCISE 18

1. The authors state that "subjects scoring high on the AIDS-WORRY scale tended to be younger." What is the numerical value of the r that supports this statement?

2. In words (not numbers) describe the direction and strength of the relationship represented by your answer to question 1.

3. Would you characterize any of the relationships, as indicated by the r's, as being "very strong"? Explain.

4. Which one of the r's represents the weakest relationship? Explain.

5. Which one of the r's represents the strongest relationship? Explain.

6. Is the relationship between age and AIDS-WORRY or the relationship between health and AIDS-WORRY stronger? Explain.

7. Did subjects who scored low on AIDS-WORRY tend to be higher or lower in rank? Explain.

8. Did subjects who reported being given guidelines tend to express higher or lower levels of worry? Explain. (Note: In the analysis, those who said they were given guidelines were assigned a score of 1, and those who said they were not were assigned a score of 0.)

9. The authors state that the high response rate reduced the chances of a serious bias. In your opinion is there still a possibility of bias? Explain.

10. The authors limited their research to only those officers working in Michigan. Are such restrictions in research justifiable? Explain.

11. Speculate on why some of the n's in Table 2 are less than 127 if 127 usable questionnaires were returned.

12. In the next to the last paragraph in the excerpt, the authors summarize the relationships shown in Table 2. In your opinion, does Table 2 add information to that provided in the paragraph or is Table 2 superfluous? Explain.

13. Based on the data, do you agree with the last sentence in the excerpt? Explain.

Notes:

EXERCISE 19

VERY-LOW-CALORIE DIET

STATISTICAL GUIDE

In simple linear regression, a single straight line is mathematically fitted to describe the dots on a scattergram. The equation for any straight line is $y = a + bx$, where a is the intercept (i.e., the score value where the line meets the vertical axis) and b is the slope (i.e., the rate of change or the direction and angle of the line). After a and b have been mathematically determined for a particular line, values for x can be inserted and the formula solved to obtain a predicted value on y.

Note that in the study described below, the subjects' body fat was pretested and posttested to assess the effects of a very low calorie diet. Hydrodensitometry measures body fat in water; bioelectrical impedance analysis (BIA) is an electrical measure.

EXCERPT FROM THE RESEARCH ARTICLE

Seventeen subjects (nine women and eight men) from an outpatient, hospital-based treatment program for obesity volunteered.

Within 10 days after baseline measures were obtained, the subjects began the 12-week VLCD [very-low-calorie diet] portion of the 26-week program. As part of the program, subjects were encouraged to record their intake and to exercise aerobically for at least 30 minutes, three times per week. At the end of the 12 weeks, all measurements were repeated in the laboratory.

Figure 1 demonstrates the relationship between age and percent of weight loss as fat. The correlation coefficient for this relationship was $r = -.49$.

Correlation between hydrostatic weighing and bioelectrical impedance was $r = .63$ for the 16 pretests and $r = .84$ for the 17 posttests. (Hydrostatic measurement of one male subject was not possible on the pretest because of discomfort in the water.) Correlation for the combined pretest and posttest trials ($n = 33$) was $r = .837$ (Figure 2).

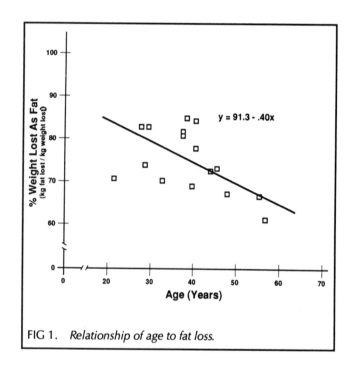

FIG 1. *Relationship of age to fat loss.*

73

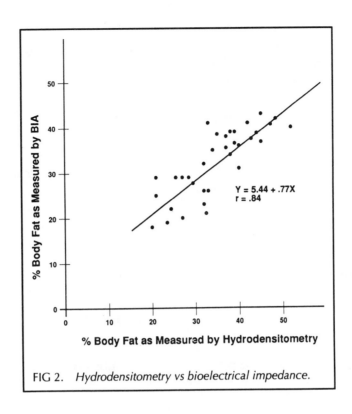

FIG 2.   *Hydrodensitometry vs bioelectrical impedance.*

SOURCE: Burgess, N. S. (1991). Effect of a very-low-calorie diet on body composition and resting metabolic rate in obese men and women. *Journal of the American Dietetic Association, 91,* 430–434. Copyright by The American Dietetic Association. Reprinted by permission.

QUESTIONS FOR EXERCISE 19

1. Is the relationship between age and percentage weight lost as fat direct or inverse? Explain.

2. In the regression analysis for age and percentage weight lost as fat, is the slope positive or negative? Explain.

3. Is the relationship depicted in Figure 1 or Figure 2 stronger? Explain.

4. At what score value will the line, if extended, meet the vertical axis (i.e., *y*-axis) in Figure 2?

74

5. Suppose you know a person whose percentage body fat as measured by hydrodensitometry is 40. Using the equation for the straight line shown in Figure 2, predict their percentage body fat as measured by BIA. (Note: Multiply 40 times the slope before adding the intercept.)

6. Suppose you know a person whose percentage body fat as measured by hydrodensitometry is 20. Use the equation to predict their percentage body fat as measured by BIA.

7. Compare your answer to questions 5 and 6 with Figure 2. Do your answers make sense? Explain.

8. Suppose you know a person whose age is 55. Using the equation for the straight line shown in Figure 1, predict the percentage of weight lost as fat that they would lose on the diet.

9. Do you think that your predictions using the information in Figure 1 or your predictions using the information in Figure 2 will be more accurate? Explain.

10. Many authors provide only the values of r and the values of a and b without showing the scattergrams (i.e., scattergrams or scatter plots) and lines as shown in the figures. Do the figures add to your understanding of the relationships and the prediction system? Explain.

11. Both axes in Figure 1 are broken with a //. This is not done in Figure 2. Why?

12. The correlation coefficient for the relationship between the two methods for measuring body fat is less than perfect. What does this tell you about the measures?

Notes:

EXERCISE 20

EXCERPTS ON SAMPLING

STATISTICAL GUIDE

In unbiased sampling, each member of a population has an equal chance of being included in the sample. Random selection is the basic method used to obtain unbiased samples. Self-selection, volunteering and any other nonrandom event (e.g., choosing people who happen to be convenient to serve as subjects) introduce bias into sampling.

QUESTIONS FOR EXERCISE 20

Directions: For each of the following excerpts, indicate whether the sample is biased or unbiased and explain your answer. In some cases, you may wish to answer "not sure" because there is insufficient information to make a judgment. If you answer "not sure" to an item, explain why.

1. Eberhardt & Pooyan (1990) reported that "surveys were mailed to a random sample of 1300 owner-operator farmers in a North Central state. A total of 362 completed surveys was received yielding a return rate of 28%."

2. Koriat, Greenberg, & Goldshmid (1991) reported that "sixty University of Haifa students (40 women, 20 men) whose native language was Hebrew participated in the experiment, 51 for course credit and the rest as volunteers."

3. Skaalvik (1990) reported that "the sample consisted of 117 boys and 114 girls from 10 sixth-grade classes in a large Norwegian city in 1988. The city was divided into four zones, and two schools were randomly drawn from each zone. One or 2 sixth-grade classes were randomly drawn from each school according to the size of the school."

4. Grimes & Swisher (1989) reported that "the subjects in this study were selected from high school students in grades 6 through 12 in 26 school districts throughout the state of Pennsylvania, which had contracted with an independent agency to conduct a survey. The subjects were stratified by grade in school and a systematized random selection technique guaranteeing a 29% sample was used to select a sample of 5,887 subjects from a total population of 29,930."

5. Klein & Keller (1990) reported that "subjects in this study were 75 seventh-grade students enrolled at the developmental research school operated by Florida State University. Students at this school are selected to be representative of Florida's school-aged population with regard to academic ability, sex, race, and socio-economic status."

6. Day & Bedeian (1991) reported that "a systematic sample was drawn from the national membership lists of the American Society of Certified Accountants, National Association of Accountants, American Association of Women Accountants, and the Association of Government Accountants. An initial name on each list was selected at random and every kth name was thereafter selected. K was computed by dividing membership list length by the desired sample size and is defined as the sampling interval."

7. Pressley, Ghatala, Woloshyn, & Pirie (1990) reported that "thirty-four Canadian undergraduate students (23 females, 11 males) who were enrolled in a first-year psychology course served as subjects in this experiment. The students' mean age was 19.4 years (range = 18–26). Subjects were randomly assigned to either the multiple-choice or the short-answer condition."

8. Aaronson (1989) reported that "the women (N = 529) were sampled from a number of private obstetricians' offices as well as from several large health centers including those with nurse-midwifery clinics. All women literate in English, over 18 years of age, and appearing for a prenatal appointment on a sample selection day were eligible, unless it was their first visit or they were more than 36 weeks pregnant. Nearly 90% of those approached agreed to participate in the study. Of these, approximately 80% returned completed questionnaires."

9. Mak (1990) reported that "subjects were 793 8th- to 12th-grade students, under the age of 18, recruited from nine government schools located in various regions in Canberra, Australia. The schools were considered by the local schools' authority to present a range of academic performance and socioeconomic background. There were 405 male and 388 female students. Their mean age was 15.63 years, with a standard deviation of 1.21 years."

10. Chappell (1991) reported that "data for this study came from a stratified random sample of persons aged 60 and over living in the community in Winnipeg, Manitoba. With assistance from the Manitoba Health Services Commission, the organization responsible for all health insurance claims (health insurance is universal in Manitoba), the sample was stratified by living arrangements. The final sample included 301 who were married and living with their spouse (included here are common-law marriages), 423 who live alone, and 560 who live with someone other than a spouse. Each of these samples is random and therefore representative for that group."

11. Botuck and Turkewitz (1990) reported that "subjects were 72 children and adolescents of average intellect, 42 girls and 30 boys, who were pupils in racially integrated Catholic schools in a working-class New York City neighborhood. There were 24 subjects in each of three groups of 7-, 13-, and 17-year-olds. Within each age and gender category, subjects were randomly selected from a list of names of pupils with school grade averages between B- and B+, who had no recorded behavior problems and no recorded physical or sensory limitations."

SOURCES: (In the order cited above.)

Eberhardt, B. J. & Pooyan, A. (1990). Development of the farm stress survey: Factorial structure, reliability, and validity. *Educational and Psychological Measurement, 50,* 393–402.

Koriat, A., Greenberg, S. N., & Goldshmid, Y. (1991). The missing-letter effect in Hebrew: Word frequency or word function? *Journal of Experimental Psychology: Learning, Memory and Cognition, 17,* 66–80.

Skaalvik, E. M. (1990) Gender differences in general academic self-esteem and success expectations on defined academic problems. *Journal of Educational Psychology, 82,* 593–598.

Grimes, J. D. & Swisher, J. D. (1989). Educational factors influencing adolescent decision making regarding use of alcohol and drugs. *Journal of Alcohol and Drug Education, 35,* 1–15.

Klein, J. D. & Keller, J. M. (1990). Influence of student ability, locus of control, and type of instructional control on performance and confidence. *The Journal of Educational Research, 83,* 140–146.

Day, V. D. & Bedeian, A. G. (1991). Work climate and Type A status as predictors of job satisfaction: A test of the interactional perspective. *Journal of Vocational Behavior, 38,* 39–50.

Pressley, M., Ghatala, E. S., Woloshyn, V., & Pirie, J. (1990). Sometimes adults miss the main ideas in text and do not realize it: Confidence in responses to short-answer and multiple-choice comprehension questions. *Reading Research Quarterly, 25,* 232–249.

Aaronson, L. (1989). Perceived and received support: Effects on health behavior during pregnancy. *Nursing Research, 38,* 4–9.

Mak, A. S. (1990). Testing a psychological control theory of delinquency. *Criminal Justice and Behavior, 17,* 215–230.

Chappell, N. L. (1991). Living arrangements and sources of caregiving. *Journal of Gerontology: Social Sciences, 46,* 1–8.

Botuck, S. & Turkewitz, G. (1990). Intersensory functioning: Auditory-visual pattern equivalence in younger and older children. *Developmental Psychology, 26,* 115–120.

Notes:

EXERCISE 21

NAUSEA IN BULIMIC WOMEN

STATISTICAL GUIDE

The standard error of the mean (SE_M) is a margin of error to allow for when estimating the population mean from a sample drawn at random from the population. When samples are reasonably large (n about 60 or more), we can have about 68 percent confidence that the population mean lies within an interval calculated as follows: sample mean plus/minus the SE_M. For example, if the sample mean = 50.0 and SE_M = 2.0, then we have 68 percent confidence that the population mean lies between 48 and 52; these are the limits of what is referred to as the 68 percent confidence interval. With small samples, the 68 percent rule is only approximate.

The SE_M is computed by dividing the standard deviation (unbiased estimate) by the square root of n.

EXCERPT FROM THE RESEARCH ARTICLE

Subjects were 11 women with bulimia. All had a history of bingeing and vomiting at least twice per week for at least 3 months prior to the study. Bulimic subjects reported that they had been binge eating for an average of 6.0 years (SE_M = 1.2, range = 0.5–12 years) and that they had been vomiting following bingeing for an average of 4.5 years (SE_M = 1.3; range = 0.5–10). Subjects estimated their frequency of bingeing and vomiting at 1.8 times per day (SE_M = 0.5).

The control subjects were 15 normal-weight, healthy women. All of the control subjects reported that they restricted their food intake by dieting. Beyond restricting food intake, the control subjects did not meet any of the other criteria for a diagnosis of either bulimia or anorexia nervosa. Control subjects had no reported history of either eating disorder.

Subjects ranged in age from 18 to 39 years; bulimic mean was 22.1 years (SE_M = 1.0), and the control mean was 22.9 years (SE_M = 1.6).

Cinnamon rolls were chosen as the food stimulus because they have features prototypical of binge foods. The cinnamon roll was presented to the subject, and she was informed that she would be allowed to eat the roll shortly. Six minutes later, the research assistant cut the roll and provided the subject with a rating questionnaire. The subject rated the roll's aroma and appearance, and her own hunger, using 7-point rating categories. Four minutes later (10 minutes after the roll had been presented), the subject was asked to eat one quarter of the roll. Subjects who were hesitant were encouraged to at least taste it. The subject then rated the roll's taste on a 7-point category rating scale. Approximately 20 minutes after the subject had been instructed to taste the roll, the uneaten portion of the roll was removed and weighed. Again using 7-point category scales, the subject rated her current level of hunger and the duration and severity of any nausea experienced during the study.

Some nausea was reported by subjects in both groups, but the incidence and severity differed between the groups. Nausea duration and nausea severity ratings are shown for each group in Table 1.

Table 1   Means and Standard Errors for Self-Report Ratings of Nausea by Bulimics and Controls

Nausea self-report measure	Controls		Bulimics	
	M	SE_M	M	SE_M
Nausea duration	1.3	0.1	3.1	0.6
Nausea severity	0.3	0.1	2.0	0.6

Note: For nausea duration, 1 = none, 7 = all the time. For nausea severity, 1 = very mild, 7 = very severe.

QUESTIONS FOR EXERCISE 21

1. Assuming that the bulimic women were sampled from a population at random, we would have about 68 percent confidence that the average age of bulimic women in the population is between what two values?

2. In light of the standard errors, does the difference in average age between the two groups seem important? Explain.

3. The mean nausea duration for bulimics was 3.1. Does the 68 percent confidence interval for this mean include the value of the mean for the controls? Explain.

4. Is the standard deviation (which is not given in the excerpt) for nausea duration for the controls larger or smaller in value than the standard error of the mean for this group? Explain.

5. Using the formula, the standard deviation = the standard error of the mean times the square root of n, calculate the standard deviation of nausea severity for bulimics and report your answer here.

6. In some of the earlier exercises, the authors reported the standard deviations and numbers of cases from which you could calculate the standard errors of means if you wished to do so. In this excerpt, the authors report standard errors of means and numbers of cases from which you could calculate standard deviations. Which method of reporting do you prefer? Explain.

7. The authors state the "bulimic subjects reported that they had been binge eating for an average of 6.0 years." Which average do you think the author used? Explain.

8. An approximate 95 percent interval can be obtained by first multiplying the SE_M by 2.0 and then adding and subtracting it from the mean. (Note: For large samples, use a multiplier of 1.96 for a more precise interval.) Calculate the 95 percent interval for the average age of bulimic women using a multiplier of 2.0 and report the limits of the interval here.

9. If your work is correct, your answer to question 8 should yield a larger confidence interval than your answer to question 1. Does this make sense? Explain.

10. If you have a statistics book, look up the more precise multiplier for obtaining a 95 percent confidence interval for the bulimics using the t table and a df of n - 1. Use the two-tailed values. Write the multiplier here.

11. If you have a statistics book, look up the more precise multiplier for obtaining a 99 percent confidence interval for the bulimics using the t table and a df of n - 1. Use the two-tailed values. Write the multiplier here.

12. If your work is correct, the multiplier you wrote as an answer to question 11 should be larger than the one for question 10. Does this make sense? Explain.

Notes:

EXERCISE 22

CUSTOMER WEIGHT AND SALESPERSONS' RESPONSE TIME

STATISTICAL GUIDE

The *t* test is often used to test the reliability (i.e., significance) of the difference between two means. The *p* value yielded by the *t* test indicates the probability that chance or random sampling errors account for the observed difference between the means. The lower the probability, the more significant the difference. Most investigators require a *p* of .05 or less before declaring a difference to be significant.

Note that "s" in the following excerpt is an abbreviation for "second" or "seconds."

EXCERPT FROM THE RESEARCH ARTICLE

One of two weight categories was assigned to all customers, "fat" or "nonfat." Response time was calculated from the moment the customer stepped into a shoe store until a salesperson approached him or her with an offer of assistance. Observations were made in an urban shopping mall at two separate shoe stores. Data were collected during 15-min intervals on four consecutive Saturday afternoons.

As a customer stepped into the store, one of the raters, who stood outside the store in an area of the mall walkway, set a stopwatch and began timing. The other two raters, one of whom stood inside the store and the other outside, assessed whether the customer was to be placed in the fat or nonfat category. If the customer was considered fat, a hand signal was given to indicate this, with no signal indicating nonfat. Both raters were required to agree upon the customer's weight category in order for the customer to be included in the study. Therefore, several customer evaluations were discarded due to lack of agreement between raters. In addition, customer evaluations were discarded if the salespersons were occupied before the customer entered the store, which would have forced the customer to wait. This left a pooled sample (fat and nonfat) of 181 observations.

There was a significant difference in response times to the fat and nonfat groups. An independent *t* test showed that the mean response time to the nonfat groups was 16.61 s, whereas that to the fat group was 29.67 s ($t = 5.38$, $p < .05$). The findings support the essentially negative evaluation of overweight individuals in our country, with fat customers experiencing longer response times from salespersons than their thinner counterparts.

SOURCE: Pauley, L. L. (1989). Customer weight as a variable in salespersons' response time. *The Journal of Social Psychology, 129,* 713–714. Reprinted with permission of the Helen Dwight Reid Educational Foundation. Published by Heldref Publications, 4000 Albemarle St., N.W., Washington, D.C. 20016. Copyright 1989.

QUESTIONS FOR EXERCISE 22

1. What was the average response time to the fat group?

2. On the average, how many seconds faster was the response time to nonfat subjects than to fat subjects?

3. What was the total number of subjects on which the t test was based?

4. What is the probability that the difference between the means was created by random sampling errors?

5. Suppose that p equals exactly .05. What would this mean? (Circle one.)

   A. 5 out of 10.   B. 5 out of 100.   C. 5 out of 1,000.   D. 1 out of 5.   E. 5 out of 1.

6. Has the author implied that the difference between the means is a reliable one? Explain.

7. The author did not report the standard deviations. Would these be of interest to you? Explain.

8. The author used an "independent" t test. If you have a statistics text, look this up and describe when it is appropriate to use an "independent" test.

9. The degrees of freedom (*df*) used in obtaining the value of *p* are not reported. If you have a statistics text, look up the formula for *df*, compute it for this study, and write your answer here.

10. In your opinion, does the elimination of some of the evaluations of some of the subjects seem reasonable? Explain.

11. Do you agree with the author's conclusion, which is stated in the last sentence? Explain.

12. Do the results of this study surprise you? Explain.

Notes:

EXERCISE 23

NINTH GRADE STUDENTS IN JUNIOR AND SENIOR HIGH

STATISTICAL GUIDE

The null hypothesis states that an observed difference is the result of random sampling errors. When a t test yields a value of t that corresponds to a low p value, the null hypothesis is rejected and the difference is declared to be statistically significant. The lower the probability, the more significant the difference because the value of p indicates the probability that random errors account for the difference.

EXCERPT FROM THE RESEARCH ARTICLE

[The] following operational null hypotheses were investigated: There will be no significant difference between (1) the mean number of extracurricular activities in which ninth-grade students in junior high schools (grades 7–9) and ninth-grade students in senior high schools (grades 9–12) participated; (2) the overall academic achievement (grade point average) means of ninth-grade students in junior and senior high schools; [and] (3) the mean attitude toward self and school of ninth-grade students in junior and senior high schools.

One intact ninth-grade classroom from each of 31 (out of a total of 38) Mississippi junior high schools ($N = 771$) and one intact ninth-grade classroom from each of 33 (out of a total of 62) Mississippi senior high schools ($N = 825$) participated in the study.

Table 1 contains the results of the analysis of hypotheses 1–3, which are summarized as follows: (1) Ninth graders in the junior high schools participated in significantly more extracurricular activities ($M = 2.68$) than did those in the senior high schools ($M = 1.99$), $p < .01$. (2) Ninth graders in the junior high schools achieved significantly higher GPAs ($M = 2.59$) than did those in the senior high schools ($M = 2.24$), $p < .01$. (3) There was no significant difference in attitudes toward self and school between ninth graders in the junior high schools ($M = 77.87$) and those in the senior high schools ($M = 78.12$), $p > .05$.

Table 1   A Comparison of the Means for Total Extracurricular Activities, Overall GPA, and Attitude Toward Self and School for Ninth Graders in Junior High ($n = 771$) and Senior High Settings ($n = 825$).

Groups	M	SD	t
Extracurricular Activities			
Ninth Graders in JHS	2.68	2.30	6.20*
Ninth Graders in SHS	1.99	2.14	
Overall GPA			
Ninth Graders in JHS	2.59	.89	6.91*
Ninth Graders in SHS	2.24	1.11	
Attitude Toward Self and School			
Ninth Graders in JHS	77.87	8.07	.60
Ninth Graders in SHS	78.12	8.48	

*$p < .01$

SOURCE: Gifford, V. D. & Dean, M. M. (1990). Differences in extracurricular activity participation, achievement, and attitudes toward school between ninth-grade students attending junior high school and those attending senior high school. *Adolescence, 25,* 799–802. Copyright 1990 by Libra Publishers. Reprinted with permission.

QUESTIONS FOR EXERCISE 23

1. Comment on the adequacy of the samples used by the investigators.

2. The text of the excerpt describes only highlights of the information in the table. In your opinion, should the text describe all of the details in the table or only the highlights?

3. Which group was more variable in terms of overall GPA?

4. At what probability level was the first difference in Table 1 significant?

5. What is the probability that the second difference in Table 1 was created by random errors?

6. At what probability level was the last difference in Table 1 *not* significant?

7. Was the first null hypothesis rejected? Explain.

8. Was the third null hypothesis rejected? Explain.

9. Write out in words the meaning of the phrase "$p > .05$."

10. Is the .01 or .05 level a higher (i.e., more significant) level?

11. If you have a statistics text, examine the table of critical values of t. Is a value of less than 1.0 (such as the value of .60 reported in Table 1) ever significant?

12. In your opinion, do the results reported here support the placement of ninth grade students in junior high school instead of senior high school? Explain.

Notes:

EXERCISE 24

EMOTIONAL DEVELOPMENT AND LEVELS OF EMPTINESS

STATISTICAL GUIDE

Analysis of variance can be used to test the significance of the difference between two means. (When used for this purpose, it yields the same value of p as a t test). The sum of the squares (SS), the degrees of freedom (df), and the mean squares (MS) are substeps in the calculation of F; it is usually not necessary to interpret these intermediate statistics as long as the value of p associated with F is clearly identified. The probability (i.e., p) indicates the likelihood that random errors created the difference. If p is sufficiently low, the difference is declared to be significant. Most investigators use p values of .05 or less as the values at which significance is declared.

The analysis of variance reported in Table 3 below is for the comparison of the mean emptiness score of 2.5 for those at level one of emotional development and the mean of 3.6 at level two.

EXCERPT FROM THE RESEARCH ARTICLE

The 61 subjects were men, ranging in age from 18 to 38 yr. old; all were diploma students in a technical institute in a large midwestern city. All had high school diplomas, 6 had associate degrees, and 1 had a baccalaureate. Fifty were single, 8 married, 2 divorced, and 1 separated.

The questionnaire to measure experienced levels of emptiness and existential concern . . . , the definition/response instrument to measure level of emotional development . . . , and a brief demographic questionnaire were administered, in that order.

It was hypothesized that levels of experiences of emptiness, existential concern, and depression will increase with emotional development.

Sixteen subjects were assigned level one of emotional development while 43 were at level two, and 2 were at level three. The averages for Experienced Levels of Emptiness, Existential Concern, and Depression by level of development are shown in Table 2.

Analysis of variance showed that only the difference between mean Experienced Levels of Emptiness at the first and second levels of emotional development was significant; see Table 3.

While this study has limitations, it does support the notion that the conscious experience of emptiness is related to observed level of development as measured.

Table 2   Means of Emptiness, Depression, and Existential Concern by Emotional Development

Level	n	Emptiness		Existential Concern		Depression	
		M	SD	M	SD	M	SD
One	16	2.5	.9	7.0	.6	2.2	3.0
Two	43	3.6	2.0	7.3	2.7	2.5	.1
Three	2	2.8	1.5	6.7	.7	2.3	1.1

Table 3   Analysis of Variance: Experienced Levels of Emptiness at Levels One and Two

Source	SS	df	MS	F
Level of Emotional Development	13.5	1	13.5	4.8*
Level of Emptiness, Error	161.5	57	2.8	
Total	175.0	58		

*$p < .05$

SOURCE: Reprinted with permission of author and publisher from Hazell, C. G. (1989). Levels of emotional development with experienced levels of emptiness and existential concern. *Psychological Reports, 64*, 835–838.

QUESTIONS FOR EXERCISE 24

1. Is the number of subjects at the highest level of emotional development (i.e., level three) adequate? Explain.

2. Does the data support the hypothesis that "depression will increase with increased emotional development"? Explain.

3. According to Table 2, which group had the greatest amount of variability in their emptiness scores?

4. What is the size of the difference between the mean emptiness scores for subjects at levels one and two of emotional development?

5. Examine the means in Table 2. Do the levels of emptiness, depression, and existential concern consistently increase across the levels of emotional development? Explain.

6. What is the probability that the value of F reported in Table 3 would be obtained as a result of random errors?

7. Has the author concluded that the difference between the means tested in Table 3 is significant at the .05 level?

8. The implied null hypothesis underlying Table 3 says that the difference between the means is the result of random errors (i.e., there is no *true* difference). What decision has the author made about this hypothesis? Explain.

9. The mean squares are obtained by dividing the corresponding sum of squares by the degrees of freedom. Check the author's calculations. Are they correct?

10. The value of F is calculated by dividing the value of the MS for emotional development by the value of the MS for Error. Check the author's calculations. Are they correct?

11. The author mentions "limitations." Are any evident in the excerpt? Explain.

Notes:

EXERCISE 25

SUBJECTS IN A STUDY OF SCHIZOPHRENIA

STATISTICAL GUIDE

Analysis of variance (ANOVA) may be used to test the differences among two or more means. Using the value of F and the degrees of freedom that are shown in parentheses in the excerpt, an investigator can use a table to determine the probability that a set of differences was created by random errors.

See the three previous statistical guides for more information on significance testing.

BACKGROUND NOTE

The excerpt below describes the subjects used in a study of schizophrenia. The normals (also referred to as the "social validation group") were subjects who lived in the same community as the psychiatric subjects. The chronic mental illness (CMI) group had mental illnesses other than schizophrenia.

EXCERPT FROM THE RESEARCH ARTICLE

Subjects for this study were solicited from a large halfway house, informed about the specifics of the study, and told that refreshments would be provided for individuals who completed all facets of the evaluation. Fifty-seven subjects consented to participate, of which 49 provided usable test batteries.

The age at testing, education, chronicity, and age at first hospitalization of subjects in the three diagnostic and social validation groups are summarized in Table 1. A one-way ANOVA showed that the four groups did not differ in age at testing, $F(3, 51) = 1.85$, $p = .152$. Education was included as a measure of both academic achievement and social competence. The psychiatric and normal groups differed in education level, with the normal group having far more education, $F(3, 54) = 20.54$, $p < .0001$. However, the three diagnostic groups [excluding normals] on education showed no difference, $F(2, 36) = 1.77$, $p = .186$. Moreover, the three diagnostic groups did not differ significantly from one another on chronicity, $F(2, 36) = 2.06$, $p = .145$, or age at first hospitalization, $F(2, 36) = 1.61$, $p = .273$.

Table 1   Description of the Samples in the Study

	Age		Education		Chronicity: Years since first hospitalization		Age at first hospitalization	
	M	SD	M	SD	M	SD	M	SD
Normals	32.6	10.8	17.1	1.0	0.0	0.0		
Nonparanoid schizophrenics	39.1	10.1	11.7	2.1	10.8	5.6	26.1	8.5
Paranoid schizophrenics	37.7	9.9	13.3	2.7	13.3	5.3	24.0	6.2
Other CMI	43.2	13.1	12.4	2.5	7.2	7.3	31.6	8.1

SOURCE: Corrigan, P. W., Davies-Farmer, R. M., & Stolley, M. R. (1990). Social cue recognition in schizophrenia under variable levels of arousal. *Cognitive Therapy and Research, 14,* 353-361. Copyright 1990 by Plenum Publishing Corporation. Reprinted with permission.

1. The authors state that the four groups did not differ in age. However, Table 1 shows differences in age. What is the explanation for this apparent discrepancy?

2. At what level was the difference in education among the four groups statistically significant?

3. Is the level that you mentioned in response to question 2 a very high level? Explain.

4. Does the significance of the difference in education among the four groups seem reasonable in light of the statistics in Table 1? Explain.

5. Which of the following most clearly and directly provides the reader with support for the assertion that the three diagnostic groups did not differ statistically on education? (Circle one.)

   A. $F = 1.77$.　B. $df = 2, 36$.　C. $p = .186$.

6. Examine your statistics text for commonly used significance levels (i.e., probability levels). Is the authors' decision to declare the differences in chronicity to be nonsignificant appropriate in light of the levels mentioned in your text? Explain.

7. Is the variation among the groups in age at testing (as indicated by the means) large compared with the variation in age within the groups (as indicated by the standard deviations)? Explain.

8. Examine your statistics text to determine whether it would have been more appropriate to use a t test instead of ANOVA to test for the significance of the differences among the four means on education. Write your findings here.

9. Review the meaning of the null hypothesis in your statistics text. Have the authors rejected the null hypothesis for the differences on age at first hospitalization? Explain.

10. Speculate on why the mean and standard deviation for one of the samples is missing in Table 1.

11. For the purposes of their study, the authors wanted diagnostic groups that were similar in terms of demographics such as age but different in their diagnoses. In your opinion, are the diagnostic groups similar in terms of demographics?

12. The authors state that the subjects were informed about the specifics of the study? Are there advantages and disadvantages in doing this? Explain.

Notes:

EXERCISE 26

USE OF RATIONALIZATION AND DENIAL

STATISTICAL GUIDE

In the excerpt, two main effects were tested: (1) the mean of all the scores for those who read the accident story versus the mean of all the scores for those who read the illness story and (2) the set of differences between the three overall means for the types of rationalization, ignoring the type of trauma. The interaction between type of trauma and use of defense mechanisms was also tested; the interaction effect answers the question of whether the differences in the use of the three types of defense mechanisms have the same pattern for the accident version as the pattern for the illness version.

There is one implied null hypothesis for each main effect and for the interaction. In each case, the null hypothesis says that the observed difference(s) are not true (i.e., they were caused by random errors).

BACKGROUND NOTE

In Figure 1, the lines for "denial" and "repression" are so close that they almost appear as a single line. In other words, the results for denial and repression are almost identical.

EXCERPT FROM THE RESEARCH ARTICLE

Each subject read a story depicting a protagonist experiencing the death of a parent, either through terminal illness (cancer) or as the result of an unexpected (auto) accident. After reading the story, the subject filled out a questionnaire designed to measure general levels of death anxiety, and then a second questionnaire designed to measure defense-mechanism use. In the second questionnaire, 6 questions measured the use of rationalization (e.g., "To what extent is the parent better off dying?"), 6 measured denial (e.g., "How likely is it that anyone you know will ever die this way?"), and 6 measured repression (e.g., "How much suffering did the victim experience?"--when the details of the story made it clear that a great deal of suffering was encountered). Responses consisted of giving a rating between 1 and 7. Higher numbers [indicate] greater defense-mechanism use. The subjects were randomly assigned to either the accident or the illness condition.

Figure 1 shows the mean defense scores as a function of both type of trauma (accident or illness) and type of defense (rationalization, denial, or repression). A mean score for each defense mechanism was computed for each subject. The points on the figure represent means across subjects. Rationalization is used with greater magnitude than either denial or repression, with the latter two yielding almost identical scores. This pattern interacts strongly with type of trauma: The difference between rationalization and the other defenses is extremely large for the accident but almost nonexistent for the illness. A 2 x 3 analysis of variance showed a main effect for type of defense mechanism [$F(2,58) = 54.8, p < .001$] and an interaction between defense mechanism and trauma [$F(2,58) = 46.2, p < .01$]. There was no effect of type of trauma ($F < 1$).

The results suggest some specific relationships between types of trauma and the types of defense mechanisms used to cope with such traumas. Rationalization is used to a much greater extent than denial or repression to cope with the accident story. For an illness, the three mechanisms are used to an extent that is virtually identical. This suggests that defense-mechanism use is specialized.

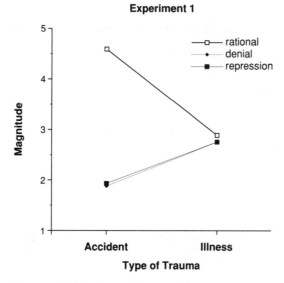

Figure 1. Magnitude of defense mechanism use as a function of type of trauma and type of defense mechanism: Experiment 1.

SOURCE: Gershuny, B. S. & Burrows, D. (1990). The use of rationalization and denial to reduce accident-related and illness-related death anxiety. *Bulletin of the Psychonomic Society, 28,* 161–163. Copyright 1990. Reprinted by permission of the Psychonomic Society, Inc.

QUESTIONS FOR EXERCISE 26

1. Does Figure 1 suggest a dramatic difference between the use of denial and repression? Explain.

2. The authors state that the analysis of variance showed a main effect for type of defense mechanism. Using the information in Figure 1, describe this main effect.

3. At what probability level was the interaction between trauma and defense mechanism declared to be significant?

4. Have the authors rejected the null hypothesis for the interaction? Explain.

5. In Figure 1, all three lines would be perfectly parallel (but not necessarily overlapping) if there was no observed interaction. Do they appear to be parallel in Figure 1? Explain.

6. The authors state that there was no effect due to type of trauma. What decision have the authors made about the associated null hypothesis?

7. For the decision regarding the main effect of type of trauma, the authors report that $F < 1$. If you have a statistics textbook, examine it to find out if an F of less than one is ever significant. Write your findings here.

8. In the last paragraph, are the authors discussing main effects or the interaction? Explain.

9. The authors assigned subjects at random to either the accident or illness condition. Was this a good idea? Explain.

10. What information in the excerpt do you find the most interesting or surprising? Explain.

Notes:

EXERCISE 27

KNOWLEDGE OF SEXUALLY TRANSMITTED DISEASES

STATISTICAL GUIDE

In a 2 x 2 x 3 ANOVA, subjects are classified according to three variables; in the following excerpt, they were classified according to two levels of sex, two levels of ethnicity, and three levels of age. The results on *main effects* indicate whether there are significant differences among the levels for each of the classification variables. These tests are interpreted in the same way as the effects in one-way ANOVAs.

The results for *interactions* indicate whether the classification variables significantly interact. In the following excerpt, there is one significant interaction; carefully studying the author's description of it will help you understand interactions.

EXCERPT FROM THE RESEARCH ARTICLE

Sixty Mexican-American male and female migrant farmworkers 18 to 35 years of age and 60 North American Black male and female migrant farmworkers 18 to 35 years of age, were selected by convenience as subjects. Both groups were stratified to include 10 males and 10 females between 18 and 23 years of age, 10 males and 10 females between 24 and 29 years of age, and 10 males and 10 females between 30 and 35 years of age.

The author designed the interview schedule consisting of 22 true-false and open-ended questions about six categories of [Sexually Transmitted Disease] STD knowledge: prevention, etiology, transmission, symptoms, treatment, and complications. Most categories contained several questions. A total score was obtained by totaling all correct responses in each category.

The majority (72%) of North American Blacks were single, divorced, or separated, while the majority (85%) of Mexican-Americans were married. Both ethnic groups had similar income distributions. The North American Blacks were more educated than the Mexican-Americans; 77% had some high school or beyond, while only 23% of the Mexican-Americans did.

The total mean STD knowledge score for the sample was 13.53 out of a possible 22 (62%). The total mean score for Blacks was 16.0 (or 72%), while the total mean score for Mexican-Americans was 11.07 (or 50%). (See Table 2). A three-way analysis of variance showed no age differences in knowledge, but ethnicity was statically significant $[F(1,108) = 44.16, p<.01]$. (See Table 3.)

Table 2   Total Mean Knowledge of Sexually Transmitted Disease by Age, Sex, and Ethnicity of Migrant Farmworkers

Age in Years by Sex	North American Black $n = 60$ Mean	Mexican-American $n = 60$ Mean	Total $n = 120$ Mean
Male	15.23	12.40	13.82
18—24	14.70	12.10	13.40
25—29	14.70	11.50	13.10
30—35	16.30	13.60	14.95
Female	16.77	9.73	13.25
18—24	16.30	9.50	12.90
25—29	16.60	11.00	13.80
30—35	17.40	8.70	13.05
Total	16.00	11.07	13.53

There was an interaction between sex and ethnicity $[F = (1,108), p<.01]$. The difference between

North American Blacks and Mexican-Americans was greater for females ($M = 16.77$ versus $M = 9.73$) than for males ($M = 15.23$ versus $M = 12.40$).

The North American Blacks in this sample had more knowledge of STDs than the Mexican-Americans. It seems likely that the difference is explained by demographic, life-style, educational, health care utilization, and cultural differences between the groups.

Table 3   Analysis of Variance in Knowledge of Sexually Transmitted Disease by Sex, Ethnicity, and Age of Migrant Farmworkers

Source of Variation	SS	df	MS	F	p
Main Effects					
Sex	9.63	1	9.63	0.58	0.45
Ethnicity	730.13	1	730.13	44.16	0.01
Age	14.87	2	7.43	0.45	0.64
2-Way Interactions					
Sex/Ethnicity	132.30	1	132.30	8.00	0.01
Sex/Age	33.87	2	16.93	1.02	0.36
Ethnicity/Age	9.27	2	4.63	0.28	0.77
3-Way Interactions					
Sex/Ethnicity/Age	16.20	2	8.10	0.49	0.61
Residual	1785.60	108	16.52		
Total	2731.86	119	22.96		

SOURCE: Smith, L. S. (1988). Ethnic differences in knowledge of sexually transmitted diseases in North American Black and Mexican-American migrant farmworkers. *Research in Nursing and Health, 11*, 51-58. Copyright 1988 by John Wiley & Sons, Inc. Reprinted by permission.

QUESTIONS FOR EXERCISE 27

1. What is the value of the difference between the mean for all of the males and the mean for all of the females? (Note: This is the main effect for sex.)

2. What is the probability that the difference referred to in question 1 was created by random errors? Did this probability lead the author to conclude that the difference was significant?

3. What is the value of the difference between the mean for all Blacks and the mean for all Mexican-Americans?

4. Does your answer to question 3 refer to a main effect or an interaction?

5. At what probability level is the difference in question 3 statistically significant?

6. In which column in Table 2 are the means that were tested for the main effect of age reported?

7. Was the null hypothesis that says that there are no true differences among the means for the main effect of age rejected? Explain.

8. Of the interactions reported in Table 3, which one has the lowest value of p associated with it?

9. Consider the following means from Table 2, and describe in words (without using numbers) the pattern of differences. (Note: If your answer is correct, you are describing an interaction.)

	Black	Mexican-American
Male	15.23	12.40
Female	16.77	9.73

10. Was the interaction that you described in question 9 statistically significant? If yes, describe the interaction.

Notes:

EXERCISE 28

EFFORT AND REWARD IN COLLEGE

STATISTICAL GUIDE

For a correlation coefficient based on data for a sample randomly drawn from a population, the null hypothesis states that the observed value is a chance deviation from a true value of 0 in the population. When the probability that the null hypothesis is true equals 5 or less in 100, most investigators declare the coefficient to be statistically significant (i.e., reliable). The lower the probability, the more significant the relationship is.

Review the statistical guides for exercises 16 through 18 before attempting this exercise.

EXCERPT FROM THE RESEARCH ARTICLE

[In an earlier study,] Schuman et al. (1985) found virtually no correlation between study time during the weekdays and GPA, a moderate but consistent correlation between study time during weekends and GPA, and a strong correlation between class attendance (or absences) and GPA. Although the association between attendance and GPA is not unexpected, the size of the correlation relative to that between study time and GPA is a surprise, as is the fact that study time on the weekend seems to be more important than study time during weekdays.

[In the present study,] students in three sections of Introduction to Sociology taught by this researcher were administered a questionnaire containing several items about study time, in addition to various kinds of other items. Of the total of seventy-three students enrolled in the three sections (excluding those who had dropped or had stopped attending) sixty students were present and took part in the survey. Participation was voluntary and no one refused to participate. The most important correlations resulting from this investigation are presented in Table 1. Table 1 reveals that the three major patterns found in the study by Schuman et al. were replicated in this investigation.

Table 1   Intercorrelations *(r)* among GPA and Predictor Variables for Three Sections of Introduction to Sociology[a]

	(1)	(2)	(3)	(4)	(5)	(6)	(7)	(8)
GPA (1)	-	.45***	.65***	.72***	.70***	.00	.30**	-.39**
HSGPA (2)		-	.52***	.32***	.37***	.06	.16	-.01
SYNGRADE (3)			-	.86***	.81***	.02	.29*	-.50***
FINAL (4)				-	.83***	-.11	.31*	-.51***
EXAM1 (5)					-	-.13	.26*	-.37**
STUDYDAY (6)						-	.17	-.01
STUDYEND (7)							-	.00
ABSENCES (8)								-

[a]Abbreviations: GPA = reported overall college Grade Point Average
HSGPA = reported High School Grade Point Average
SYNGRADE = semester grade in Sociology course
FINAL = score on comprehensive Final in Sociology
EXAM1 = score on first exam in Sociology
STUDYDAY = estimated average number of hours studied during weekdays
STUDYEND = estimated average number of hours studied on weekends
ABSENCES = actual number of absences in the Sociology course

Correlations involving SYNGRADE are based on N = 58; correlations involving FINAL on N = 55; All other correlations based on N = 60.

*.05 level of significance; **.01 level of significance; ***.001 level of significance.

SOURCE: Hill, L. (1990). Effort and reward in college: A replication of some puzzling findings. *Handbook of Replication Research in the Behavioral and Social Sciences,* A Special Issue of the *Journal of Social and Behavior Personality, 5,* 151–161. Copyright 1990 by Select Press. Reprinted with permission.

QUESTIONS FOR EXERCISE 28

1. Which variable correlates most highly with GPA?

2. Which variable had the lowest correlation with GPA?

3. Describe in words (without using numbers) the strength and direction of the relationship between hours studied during weekdays and hours studied during weekends.

4. Based on the statistics in Table 1, would a student who had many absences most likely have a high or low final exam score? Explain.

5. Absences had significant correlations with which four variables?

6. Is the relationship between hours studied during weekdays and scores on the final exam statistically significant?

7. Has the null hypothesis for the relationship between college GPA and hours studied on weekends been rejected?

8. Which variable stands out because of its consistent lack of significant correlation with the other variables?

9. At what probability level was the relationship between college GPA and high school GPA declared to be significant?

10. Is the relationship between variables 4 and 7 significant at a higher or lower level than the relationship between variables 4 and 8?

11. At first glance, the intercorrelation table seems to be incomplete because there are no values in the bottom left-hand half of the table. Is it actually incomplete? Explain.

12. The estimated number of hours studied was determined by administering a self-report questionnaire. Are there advantages and disadvantages to using such an instrument? Explain.

Notes:

EXERCISE 29

NON-VERBAL INTELLIGENCE MEASURES

STATISTICAL GUIDE

The significance of the difference between two correlation coefficients can be determined with a t test. A significant result indicates that the difference is reliable and that the associated null hypothesis is to be rejected.

In the following excerpt, the authors report on the significance of individual coefficients (see the guide for the previous exercise) as well as the significance of the differences between pairs of variables.

BACKGROUND NOTES

The *Wechsler Adult Intelligence Scale-Revised* (WAIS-R) is a popular measure of intelligence that includes a non-verbal section called the Performance Tests. The *Hiskey-Nebraska Test of Learning Aptitude* (H-NTLA) is a non-verbal measure of intelligence designed specifically for use with deaf examinees. An important function of intelligence tests is predicting achievement.

In the excerpt, an age of 16-1 means 16 years and one month old.

EXCERPT FROM THE RESEARCH ARTICLE

A familiar and often frustrating decision facing psychological evaluators in working with deaf clients is choosing an appropriate tool to assess non-verbal intelligence.

The authors hypothesized, based on clinical experience, that the Performance Scale of the WAIS-R correlated higher with achievement in deaf adolescents than the H-NTLA.

Subjects were 35 deaf adolescents (20 females and 15 males) aged 16-1 to 18-0 years who were students at the residential school for the deaf in Arkansas.

The achievement test scores were from the *Stanford Achievement Test, Special Edition for the Hearing Impaired* in reading comprehension and mathematical computation.

Scores on the H-NTLA ranged from 40 to 103 with a mean of 79; on the Wechsler Performance from 58 to 126 with a mean of 90; on the Stanford reading comprehension from 2 to 99 with a mean of 54.4; and on the Stanford math computation from 2 to 88 with a mean of 48.9.

The results of the analysis using the Pearson Product-Moment correlation are shown in Table 1. These correlation coefficients were all significant at the $p < .01$ level of confidence. Further, one-tailed t-tests for the significance of the differences between dependent correlations showed that the WAIS-R Performance Scale correlated higher with reading comprehension than did the H-NTLA ($t = 2.38$; $df = 32$; $p < .05$). There was no significant difference between the WAIS-R Performance Scale and the H-NTLA in their correlations with mathematical calculations. We also computed the correlation between the H-NTLA and the WAIS-R Performance Scale and found that these two instruments were significantly correlated ($r = .75$; $p < .01$).

Table 1

Achievement Measure	H-NTLA	WAIS-R
SAT-Reading Comprehension	.53*	.73*
SAT-Mathematical	.60*	.70*

*$p < .01$

SOURCE: Paal, N., Skinner, S., & Reddig, C. (1988). The relationship of non-verbal intelligence measures to academic achievement among deaf adolescents. *Journal of Rehabilitation of the Deaf, 21,* 8–11. Copyright 1988 by The American Deafness and Rehabilitation Association. Reprinted with permission.

1. Describe in words (without using numbers) the direction and strength of the relationship between WAIS-R Performance scores and SAT-Reading Comprehension scores.

2. According to Table 1, the relationship between which two variables is strongest?

3. According to Table 1, the relationship between which two variables is weakest?

4. Is the relationship between H-NTLA and WAIS-R Performance statistically significant? Explain.

5. Is the difference between $r = .53$ and $r = .73$ in Table 1 statistically significant? Explain.

6. Has the null hypothesis for the difference in question 5 been rejected? Explain.

7. Is the difference between $r = .60$ and $r = .70$ in Table 1 statistically significant? Explain.

8. Has the null hypothesis for the difference in question 7 been rejected? Explain.

9. Do you believe that the authors' hypothesis has been supported by the data? Explain.

10. Speculate on what the authors mean by "dependent correlations."

11. The authors stated that they used one-tailed t tests. If you have a statistics textbook, look up this term and define it here.

12. The authors have not given Table 1 a caption (i.e., title). Using the captions for other tables in this book as models, write a title for Table 1.

Notes:

EXERCISE 30

PERCEIVED STRESS LEVELS

STATISTICAL GUIDE

The correlation coefficients (the values of *r*) in Table 1 indicate the extent to which pairs of variables are correlated.

A multiple correlation coefficient (*R*) indicates the extent to which a combination of variables predict one other variable (in this case, physical symptoms). Often, predictors that are good predictors individually do not predict much better in combination with each other.

Squaring *R* yields the coefficient of determination, which may be thought of as the proportion of variance in the criterion or dependent variable that is being predicted by the combination; this is sometimes referred to as the *variance accounted for* in the criterion variable; this variance is sometimes called *explained variance* or *common variance*.

EXCERPT FROM THE RESEARCH ARTICLE

Specifically, it was hypothesized that law enforcement supervisors reporting higher levels of perceived stress would report a greater incidence of physical symptoms as compared to those experiencing lower levels of stress.

Subjects were 139 middle-level supervisory personnel employed by a large state law enforcement organization.

The *Cohen-Hoberman Inventory of Physical Symptoms (CHIPS)* (Cohen and Hoberman, 1982) is a list of 39 common physical symptoms which are rated for how bothersome or distressing they were to the individual during the past two weeks (5-point scale from "not at all" to "extremely") yielding a single overall score. The *Perceived Stress Scale (PSS)* (Cohen, Kamarck, and Mermelstein, 1983) is a 14-item self-report measure designed to measure the degree to which an individual generally perceives his or her life as stressful. Subjects respond using a 0-4 scale (0 = never, 4 = very often) to questions such as "In the last month, how often have you felt confident about your ability to handle your personal problems?" The *Job Descriptive Index (JDI)* (Smith, Kenall, and Julin, 1969) is a 74-item self-report measure of job satisfaction. It contains five subscales. Resting blood pressure (diastolic and systolic) was also assessed via sphygmomanometer on the same day the subjects completed the above inventory.

Correlational stepwise regression analyses were performed to identify the relationship between self-reported physical symptoms (CHIPS), perceived stress (PSS), job satisfaction (JDI), and blood pressure. As

Table 1   Correlation between Physical Symptoms (CHIPS), Perceived Stress (PSS), Job Satisfaction, and Blood Pressure

	PSS	CHIPS	DBP	SBP
JDI Subscales, Satisfaction with				
Nature of Work	-.35**	-.44**	.09	.01
Supervisors	-.14	-.23*	.23	.10
Interpersonal Interactions	-.24*	-.25*	.06	.08
Pay	.03	-.09	.04	-.05
Promotional Opportunities	-.20	-.21*	-.05	-.04
JDI (total)	-.29**	-.36**	.10	.04
PSS	—	.45**	-.16	-.12
Diastolic Blood Pressure (DBP)	-.16	-.16	—	.42**
Systolic Blood Pressure (SBP)	-.12	-.03	.42**	—

Note: Positive scores indicate higher satisfaction with job.   *$p < .01$, **$p < .001$

expected, perceived stress was significantly correlated with physical symptoms and job dissatisfaction (see Table 1.)

The second step to data analysis was to perform a series of stepwise regression analyses to identify the combination of variables that best predicted physical symptoms. The best model for predicting physical symptoms was a two-variable model containing PSS and dissatisfaction with the nature of the work ($R^2 = .29$, $F(6,138) = 28.9$, $p < .005$) (see Table 2). The overall variance accounted for (R^2) was not significantly increased by any of the other subscales of the JDI or blood pressure.

Table 2   Prediction of Physical Symptoms

Model	Multiple R	R^2	Change in R^2
Perceived Stress	.45	.20	.20
Nature of Work	.54	.29	.09

The correlational basis of our findings precludes causal inferences between stress and physical symptoms. It is possible that increased symptomatology leads to increased stress, rather than higher stress levels influencing report of physical symptoms.

SOURCE: Norvell, N., Belles, D. & Hills, H. (1988). Perceived stress levels and physical symptoms in supervisory law enforcement personnel. *Journal of Police Science and Administration, 16*, 75-79. Copyright 1988 by the International Association of Chiefs of Police. Reprinted with permission.

QUESTIONS FOR EXERCISE 30

1. Which variable in Table 1 is the single best predictor of CHIPS?

2. Which variable in Table 1 is the second single best predictor of CHIPS?

3. Which two variables, in combination, provided the best model for predicting physical symptoms?

4. By how much did the proportion of variance accounted for increase when nature of work was combined with perceived stress in the prediction of physical symptoms?

5. Why did the authors stop with a combination of only two variables instead of using all variables in their prediction of symptoms in Table 2?

6. At what probability level was the combination of the two predictors for predicting symptoms in Table 2 significant?

7. In light of the statistics in Table 1, does it surprise you that SBP did not make a significant contribution to the prediction of symptoms in the multiple regression analysis? Explain.

8. The first change in Table 2 is .20. Speculate on what this change refers to.

9. The authors state that correlational analyses do not permit causal interpretations. If you have a statistics textbook, determine whether the author of your textbook agrees and write your findings here.

10. What information in the excerpt do you find the most interesting or surprising? Explain.

Notes:

EXERCISE 31

PAIN AND DEPRESSION

STATISTICAL GUIDE

Chi square (χ^2) tests for the reliability of differences among frequencies (or the percentages associated with frequencies).

The null hypothesis states that observed differences are merely the result of random errors. Chi square yields the probability that this hypothesis is true (i.e., that there is no true difference). When this probability (i.e., p) is small (such as $p < .05$), the differences are declared to be statistically significant (i.e., reliable). The smaller p is, the more significant the result.

EXCERPT FROM THE RESEARCH ARTICLE

Respondents were residents of a large multilevel care facility for Jewish elderly. Of the total sample of 598, 191 lived in a skilled and intermediate nursing home and 407 in high-rise congregate apartments for more able elderly at the same site. The sample was 70% female and ranged in age from 61 to 99 years.

All self-report data were gathered as part of longer interviews with each participating resident. Twelve items assessed presence or absence of *localized pain* such as headaches, intestinal or stomach pain, chest pains and joint pain.

A 35-item symptom checklist based on the *Diagnostic and Statistical Manual* revised 3rd edition (DSM-IIIR; American Psychiatric Association, 1987) assessed subjective, observed, and vegetative symptoms of depression. Responses were classified according to DSM-IIIR criteria as indicating (a) possible major depression ($n = 62$), (b) minor depression ($n = 172$), or (c) no depression ($n = 374$).

Table 2 presents frequencies with which persons displaying possible major, minor, or no depression reported presence of each of 12 specific types of pain.

Table 2   Localized Pain Complaints as a Function of Level of Depression

	Possible Major Depression (%)	Minor Depression (%)	No Depression (%)	Chi Square df = 2
Headaches	27.9	27.5	21.7	2.69
Neckaches	50.0	32.7	18.5	33.47***
Arm/leg aches or pains	69.4	45.6	33.3	30.94***
Backaches	50.0	43.9	35.7	6.20*
Stomach/intestinal pain	39.3	31.8	16.3	25.85***
Painful urination	27.9	12.9	7.1	24.05***
Hand/foot aches or pains	59.7	43.5	37.5	11.16**
Chest pain	26.2	26.9	13.2	17.27***
Skin burns/tingles/crawls	27.9	20.0	12.7	11.17**
Bone pain	43.5	22.9	13.8	31.55***
Joint pain	50.0	45.0	37.5	5.10
Muscle aches/pains	47.5	31.8	20.7	21.90***

*$p < .05$; **$p < .005$; ***$p < .001$.

SOURCE: Parmelee, P. A., Katz, I. R., & Lawton, M. P. (1991). The relation of pain to depression among institutionalized aged. *Journal of Gerontology: Psychological Sciences, 46,* 15–21. Copyright by The Gerontological Society of America. Reprinted with permission.

QUESTIONS FOR EXERCISE 31

1. Is the pattern for bone pain similar to the pattern for muscle aches/pains? Explain.

2. Were the differences for joint pain statistically significant?

3. Describe in words (without using numbers) the pattern for neckaches.

4. Are the differences referred to in question 3 statistically significant? If yes, at what level?

5. For chest pain, how many differences were analyzed by the chi-square test? Explain.

6. Was the null hypothesis regarding chest pain rejected? Explain.

7. Was the set of differences for backaches more or less significant than the set of differences for stomach/intestinal pain? Explain.

8. In Table 2, the authors state that $df = 2$. If you have a statistics textbook, look up the meaning of df and write your finding here.

9. The authors' data were collected through self-reports. Speculate on the advantages and disadvantages of using such measures.

10. Which of the three depression groups had the largest number of subjects? Explain.

11. Assume that you are writing a term paper about pain and depression among the elderly. Write a brief paraphrase of the findings of this study that you might include in your paper.

12. What information in the excerpt do you find the most interesting or surprising?

Notes:

EXERCISE 32

SCIENCE IN THE PRESSES

STATISTICAL GUIDE

See the guide for exercise 31.

BACKGROUND NOTES

Chi-square tests were used to obtain the probabilities given in Table 2. Although percentages are reported in this table, the chi-square tests were conducted on the frequencies that underlie the percentages.

By "original forum of research" the authors mean "book, article, conference paper, and so forth." By "research method" the authors mean "laboratory experiment, survey, case study, and so on." By "contextual factors" the authors mean "comments that place the research in context with prior research and comments regarding the limitations or generalizability of the research findings."

EXCERPT FROM THE RESEARCH ARTICLE

Every issue of the *New York Times, Philadelphia Inquirer, National Enquirer,* and *Star* for the month of September 1987 was analyzed in this study. Any article dealing primarily with theoretical or applied findings from behavioral, biological, chemical, physical, or social research was considered. An article was considered to deal *primarily* with science research if its major focus was on specific findings of a scientific research endeavor. Thus, an article that may merely cite a scientist, or an article that may incidentally report on the planning of scientific projects might not have been included if, overall, it did not discuss specific findings.

Each reported study was coded by one member of a team of trained coders. A randomly selected subset of reported studies (10 percent of the total sample) was coded by all coders. Intercoder agreement exceeded 82 percent on all items.

As shown in Table 2, the *Times* and *Inquirer* were, in general, more likely than the *Enquirer* and *Star* to include such details [as names and affiliations of the researchers, the original forum of the research, and

Table 2   Percentage of Research Study Reports in Prestige and National Tabloid Press by Comprehensiveness Variables

Comprehensiveness Variables	New York Times and Philadelphia Inquirer	National Enquirer and Star
Institutional affiliation of researcher specified*	97.8%	90.6%
Identification of researcher by name***	70.3	46.2
Original forum of research specified***	90.8	62.3
Research method specified	44.3	40.6
Discussion of research method**	36.2	19.8
Research placed in context***	35.1	13.2
Limitations of research noted***	15.7	1.9
	(*n* = 185)	(*n* = 106)

*p < .05.
**p < .01.
***p < .001.

the particular research method utilized, and statements regarding context and limitations] in their science reporting. However, while offering relatively more comprehensive science reporting than the national tabloids, the prestige newspapers omitted *some* relevant information in a majority of their research study reports.

(FOOTNOTE: Statistical tests are used here and throughout the paper only for heuristic purposes; no claim is made that our one-month sample is perfectly representative of all issues of all four newspapers published in 1987 or any other year. However, there is no reason to believe that our sample is in any way atypical. September 1987 was a month in which no unusual or "breaking" science stories dominated press coverage of science.)

SOURCE: Evans, W. A., Krippendorf, M., Yoon, J. H., Posluszny, P., & Thomas, S. (1990). Science in the prestige and national tabloid presses. *Social Science Quarterly, 71,* 105–117. Copyright 1990 by the University of Texas Press. Reprinted with permission.

QUESTIONS FOR EXERCISE 32

1. In your opinion, is the sample adequate?

2. What is the advantage of using a random subset of reported studies to determine intercoder agreement?

3. For the analysis in Table 2, the reports from pairs of papers were combined to form two categories of papers. In your opinion, was this a good idea? Explain.

4. Why was it important for the authors to report percentages in Table 2 instead of raw frequencies?

5. On which comprehensiveness variable was there a nonsignificant difference?

6. Was the difference associated with "institutional affiliation of researcher specified" or the one associated with "identification of researcher by name" significant at a higher level?

7. Was the null hypothesis rejected for the variable named "limitations of research noted"? Explain.

8. The term "$p < .001$" means that p is (Circle one.)
   A. less than 1 in 100.
   B. more than 1 in 100.
   C. less than 1 in 1000.
   D. more than 1 in 1000.

9. What is the probability that the difference for "research placed in context" is the result of random errors?

10. In your opinion, do the data support the authors' statements in the last paragraph of the excerpt? Explain.

11. What information in the excerpt do you find the most interesting or surprising? Explain.

Notes:

EXERCISE 33

PROBING THE PUBLIC'S HONESTY

STATISTICAL GUIDE

A chi-square (χ^2) test of homogeneity indicates the reliability (i.e., significance) of observed differences between two samples. In Table 3, the question tested by chi square is whether the populations of younger and older subjects are homogeneous (i.e., similar) with respect to their tendency to return "lost" letters. The p yielded by chi square indicates the probability that the differences are created by sampling (i.e., chance or random) errors. The lower the probability, the more significant the relationship indicated by the differences.

EXCERPT FROM THE RESEARCH ARTICLE

A total of 112 stamped, addressed, but unmailed, letters were planted securely under the windshield wipers of cars witnessed arriving and parking in various shopping center lots throughout the city [of Ottawa]. Subjects (solitary drivers) were selected so as to ensure that the sample contained an equal number of males and females under and over 30 years of age.

Fifty-six or one-half of the letters were typed on what appeared to be the official letterhead of "The Coin Collector's Association of Canada" (a fictitious organization.) Each envelope contained a penny encased in a bulky, authentic coin holder and an accompanying letter [that indicated that the coin was worth $150.00]. Fifty-six handwritten "personal" letters served as a comparison. These letters contained a trivial "thank you" note and had no urgency or value attached to them. Each of the 112 letters was coded to indicate, to the investigators, the age and sex of the subject returning it. The envelopes were only semi-sealed, to promote temptation, waylay suspicion and to provide later evidence of tampering. A scrawled note containing the message "found near your car" was also placed with each envelope under the windshield wiper of each subject's car.

Overall, 83 (74%) of the 112 "lost" letters were returned, often in a better condition (sealed, scotch-taped, etc.) than when our subjects first discovered them.

As mentioned, we dichotomized the variable of age, with the cutting-point being 30 years of age. As Table 3 indicates, 20 (36%) of the subjects under 30 years of age failed to return the "lost" letters, whereas only 9 (16%) of subjects over that age failed to do so.

Table 3 The Relationship Between the Age of the Subjects and Their Return Rate of the "Lost" Letters

	Returned	Not Returned	Total	χ^2	d.f.	p
All Letters						
Younger	36	20	56			
Older	47	9	56	5.63	1	< .02
Letters with Coin						
Younger	19	9	28			
Older	20	8	28	.09	1	n.s.*
Personal Letters						
Younger	17	11	28			
Older	27	1	28	10.60	1	< .01

*n.s. = not significant; $p > .05$

SOURCE: Gabor, T. & Tonia, B. (1989). Probing the public's honesty: A field experiment using the "lost letter" technique. *Deviant Behavior, 10,* 387–399. Copyright 1989 by Hemisphere Publishing Corporation, New York. Reprinted with permission.

QUESTIONS FOR EXERCISE 33

1. What is your opinion of the authors' decision to dichotomize the variable of age with a cutting point of 30 years?

2. For what words does "*n.s.*" stand?

3. Describe in words (without using numbers) the relationship indicated by the data in Table 3 for all letters.

4. Is the relationship that you described in question 3 statistically significant? Explain.

5. Based on your answer to question 4, should you conclude that the two populations (i.e., younger and older) are probably homogeneous with respect to returning all letters? Explain.

6. Based on the significance test, how likely is it that the relationship between age and returning letters with a coin is due to random errors?

7. Describe in words (without using numbers) the relationship indicated by the data in Table 3 for personal letters.

8. At what probability level did the relationship that you described in question 7 achieve statistical significance?

9. Which of the three significance tests yielded significance at the highest (i.e., most significant) level?

10. What is your opinion of the "lost letter" technique for measuring honesty?

11. What information in the excerpt do you find the most interesting or surprising? Explain.

Notes:

EXERCISE 34

EFFECTIVENESS OF BICYCLE SAFETY HELMETS

STATISTICAL GUIDE

Review the statistical guide for Exercise 33.

The null hypothesis states that the differences between populations are due to random (i.e., chance) sampling errors. The values of p indicate the probability that this hypothesis is true. When these values are low (usually .05 or less) investigators usually reject the null hypothesis as the explanation for the differences. Stating that the null hypothesis has been rejected is equivalent to declaring the result to be statistically significant.

EXCERPT FROM THE RESEARCH ARTICLE

The case patients were bicyclists who sought care for bicycle-related head injuries in the emergency room of one of the five hospitals. The emergency room control group consisted of bicyclists who sought care at the same emergency rooms for bicycle-related injuries other than head injuries.

Overall 7.2 percent of the case patients and 23.8 percent of the emergency room controls wore helmets. Safety helmets reduce the risk of head injury by 85 percent and brain injury by 88 percent.

Table 3   Characteristics of the Accident*

Characteristic	Case Patients		Emergency Room Controls		p value
	No.	%	No.	%	
Cause of crash					
Contact with moving motor vehicle	53	22.6	54	12.5	
Contact with other moving objects**	18	7.7	52	12.0	
Contact with stationary obstacle***	57	24.3	123	28.4	
Avoiding obstacles****	6	2.6	20	4.6	
Bicycle malfunction or unsafe bicycle*****	14	6.0	41	9.5	
Falls	87	37.0	143	33.0	0.003
Type of surface					
Paved (concrete, asphalt)	213	90.6	365	84.3	
Gravel	13	5.5	31	7.2	
Dirt or grass	9	3.8	37	8.5	0.04
Self-reported speed (mi/hr)					
Slow (<5)	74	31.5	137	31.6	
Moderate (5-15)	90	38.3	161	37.2	
Fast (>15)	52	22.1	111	25.6	
Unknown	19	8.1	24	5.5	0.8
Damage to bicycle					
No	106	45.1	232	53.6	
Yes	129	54.9	201	46.4	0.01
Damage requiring repairs					
No	131	55.7	262	60.5	
Yes	83	35.3	150	34.6	
Beyond repair	21	8.9	21	4.8	0.1

*P values indicate the significance of differences in distribution between case patients and controls by chi square analysis.
**Includes bicycles, pedestrians, and animals.
***Includes parked cars, bumps, and curbs.
****Includes cars, pedestrians, and animals.
*****Includes chain falling off, flat tire, handlebars coming off, and no seat.

SOURCE: Thompson, R. S., Rivara, F. P., & Thompson, D. C. (1989). A case-control study of the effectiveness of bicycle safety helmets. *The New England Journal of Medicine, 320,* 1361–1367. Reprinted with permission from *The New England Journal of Medicine.*

QUESTIONS FOR EXERCISE 34

1. The number of subjects who had contact with moving motor vehicles is about the same for both groups (i.e., 53 and 54). Yet, the percentages are different. Why are the percentages different if the numbers are about the same?

2. For both groups, the vast majority of accidents occurred on what type of surface?

3. Briefly describe the relationship between "Damage to bicycle" and type of subject (i.e., case patients versus controls). Describe this relationship in general terms without using numbers or percents.

4. Is the relationship that you described in response to question 3 significant at the 0.01 level? Explain.

5. Has the null hypothesis for the relationship that you described in response to question 3 been rejected? Explain.

6. Briefly describe the relationship between type of surface and type of subject. Describe this relationship in general terms without using numbers or percentages.

7. Is the relationship that you described in response to question 6 significant at the .05 level? (Note: "The .05 level" means ".05 or less.") Explain.

8. Examining the differences in percentages between the two groups on self-reported speed, do you find large, dramatic differences? Explain.

9. Has the null hypothesis for the relationship between self-reported speed and type of subject been rejected? Explain.

10. Of the five comparisons employing chi square, which one is the most statistically significant? Explain.

11. The authors chose not to report the values of chi square and the degrees of freedom on which the probabilities are based. How do you feel about their decision? Explain.

12. The authors chose to report both the number and the associated percentages for each variable. Do you believe that it would have been better to report just the percentages? Explain.

Notes:

EXERCISE 35

COMPUTER-ASSISTED INSTRUCTION

STATISTICAL GUIDE

The Wilcoxon matched-pairs signed-ranks test tests for the significance of the difference between two sets of ranks obtained from matched pairs. In the study described below, the subjects in the two groups were matched on GPA. Their SAT scores were the outcome measure; the difference between the ranks of the pairs of scores was tested for significance.

EXCERPT FROM THE RESEARCH ARTICLE

Sixteen students from a low to middle income rural high school served as subjects in Northeastern Washington. The experimental group consisted of eight self-selected 12th grade students. Every student enrolled in the school had the opportunity to participate in the computer-assisted instruction [C.A.I.] program used for the purpose of preparing them for the SAT. The control group consisted of eight randomly selected same grade peers with comparable grade point averages who were enrolled in similar classes as the students in the experimental group. Official school transcripts revealed a 3.1 or higher grade point average for both groups of students.

The actual *Scholastic Aptitude Test* (SAT) performance scores reported to the high school counseling department by the Admissions Testing Program (ATP) of the College Board were used for the purpose of measurement.

The results indicated that there was a large difference between the SAT scores of the two groups. The scores in the experimental group ranged from a low combined score of 940 to a high combined score of 1480 ($M = 1137$). This was a difference of 186 points over the control group. The control group generated scores that ranged from 710 to 1250 ($M = 951$). The results of this study suggest that computer-assisted instruction aided students in attaining higher SAT scores.

Table 1   Scores Made by Matched Pairs by Grade Point Average in the C.A.I. and Control Group

Identical Pairs by GPA	C.A.I.	Control	Difference	Rank of d	Rank of Less Frequent Sign
3.76/3.72	1480	890	590	8	
3.69/3.66	1050	800	250	5	
3.95/3.96	1220	1060	160	3	
3.24/3.27	940	760	180	4	
3.11/3.13	1140	710	430	7	
3.39/3.42	870	1250	-380	-6	6
3.47/3.51	1210	1090	120	1	
3.75/3.78	1190	1050	140	2	

Wilcoxon Matched-Pairs Signed-Ranks Test ($T = 6$, $N = 8$)

SOURCE: Fine, L. F., Bialozor, R. C., & McLaughlin, T. F. (1991). An analysis of computer-assisted instruction on Scholastic Aptitude Test performance of rural high school students. *Education, 111,* 400-403. Copyright 1991 by Project Innovation. Reprinted with permission.

QUESTIONS FOR EXERCISE 35

1. The subjects in the experimental group were volunteers. Does this complicate the interpretation of the results? Explain.

2. Is it important to know that all subjects were administered the SAT on the same date and at the same time? Explain.

3. In your opinion, are the two groups closely matched on GPA?

4. Are the two groups similar in their variability on the SAT?

5. Which group had a higher mean score?

6. For the first pair of subjects in Table 1, what is the difference between their SAT scores?

7. Why did the seventh pair of subjects in Table 1 receive a rank of 1?

8. In how many cases did a member of the control group score higher than his/her match in the experimental group?

9. If your statistics textbook has a table of critical values of T for the Wilcoxon test, use it to determine if the T of 6 reported here is significant at a level of your choice. Write your findings here, including the level you chose, whether the test was one-tailed or two-tailed, and the critical value.

10. Do you agree with the last statement in the excerpt? Explain.

11. Assume that you were planning a follow-up study on the same topic. Name any changes you would make in the research methodology.

Notes:

EXERCISE 36

NURSES' PERCEPTIONS OF CARING BEHAVIORS

STATISTICAL GUIDE

The Mann-Whitney U test is a test of statistical significance. When the resulting p value is .05 or less, the null hypothesis is usually rejected and statistical significance declared.

Ordinal data are scores that put subjects in rank order on a variable. The Mann-Whitney U is a test of the significance of the difference between two sets of ranks for independent samples.

EXCERPT FROM THE RESEARCH ARTICLE

The participants included senior baccalaureate nursing students ($n = 30$) at Thomas Jefferson University, College of Allied Health Sciences, and professional nurses who had 1 or more years experience ($n = 30$).

The 50 behavioral items are ordered in six subscales of caring. They are:

Accessible (6 items);
Explains and facilitates (6 items);
Comforts (9 items);
Anticipates (5 items);
Trusting relationship (16 items);
Monitors and follows through (8 items) (Larson, 1981, 1984).

Each participant sorted 50 CARE-Q cards into 7 different packets. Each card contained one of the 50 identified nurse care behaviors. The packets represent the range of most important to not important. The participants were instructed to sort out only 1 item as most important; 4 items as fairly important; 10 items as somewhat important; 20 items as neither important or unimportant; 10 items as somewhat unimportant; 4 as unimportant; and 1 as not important. Each participant spent approximately 45 minutes to complete the assessment.

The statistical test used to analyze the ordinal data was the Mann Whitney U test. The Mann Whitney U test is based on the assignment of ranks to the two groups of measures. The sum of the ranks for the two groups can be compared by calculating the U statistic (Polit and Hungler, 1983).

Each of the behavioral items was ordered within six subscales of caring. The data for each group (professional nurses and student nurses) were ranked for each of the subscales. The sum of the ranks for both groups for each subscale was compared by calculating the U statistic. The scores for each subscale category along with the resulting Z- and p-values are presented in Table 2.

Overall there is no significant difference between the professional nurses' perceptions of effective care

Table 2   Scores on Subscales of Caring

Subscales	Nursing Group	Student Group	Z*	p
Accessibility	906.0	924.0	-.12	0.89
Explains	874.5	955.5	-.59	0.54
Anticipates	903.5	926.5	-.16	0.86
Comforts	820.5	1009.5	-1.39	0.16
Monitors	903.0	927.0	-.17	0.86
Trusts	1041.5	788.5	1.86	0.06

*The Mann-Whitney U Test requires finding a Z-value if one of the groups is larger than 20.

behaviors and that of senior nursing students. The trust subscale category approaches significance ($p = .06$). The professional nurses ranked those items in the trusting relationship subscales higher than the nursing students.

Since there is little difference between the nurses' and students' perceptions of effective care behaviors, it may be that the perceptions develop sometime during the educational process and may differ earlier in the development of the student nurse.

SOURCE: Mangold, A. M. (1991). Senior nursing students' and professional nurses' perceptions of effective caring behaviors: A comparative study. *Journal of Nursing Education, 30*, 134–139. Copyright 1991 by SLACK Incorporated. Reprinted by permission.

QUESTIONS FOR EXERCISE 36

1. Did the sorting of statements by the subjects yield ordinal data? Explain.

2. Which group rated the items on the trust subscale as more important?

3. Which group rated the items in the comfort subscale as more important?

4. Has the author rejected the null hypothesis for the difference on the accessibility subscale?

5. What is the probability that the null hypothesis for the difference on the "explains" subscale is true?

6. The author states that the trust subscale "approaches significance." What is the basis for this statement?

7. For a two-tailed test, $\dot{Z}$ must be 1.96 or higher in value for significance at the .05 level. Are any of the Z values in Table 2 this high or higher?

8. Do you agree with the point made in the last paragraph of the excerpt? Explain.

Notes:

APPENDIX A

FEAR OF AIDS AND ATTRITION AMONG MEDICAL TECHNOLOGISTS*

Ronald R. Gauch
Fairleigh Dickinson University

Karen B. Feeney
Bayshore Community Hospital

James W. Brown
Roche Biomedical Laboratories

Abstract: Attitudes toward AIDS were measured by a survey of 212 attendees at the annual meeting of the New Jersey Society for Medical Technology. Twenty five percent of the respondents were considering leaving the profession because of a fear of AIDS. In addition, almost half would not have chosen the field knowing they would be handling HIV-positive samples. This high degree of concern may be an important factor contributing to the shortage of medical technologists.

(1) A 1988 survey by the American Society of Clinical Pathologists reported that 9 percent of medical technologists positions are vacant and more than 75 percent of laboratory managers perceive a shortage of qualified laboratory personnel.[1] The shortage among medical technologists has been attributed to a wide spectrum of problems: low pay with a compressed salary structure, lack of upward mobility, job stress, poor working conditions, lack of professional recognition, and increased opportunities in other professions that have commensurate educational requirements.[2,3]

(2) A survey conducted in 1987 among New England laboratories reported that 39 percent of the respondents mentioned fear of AIDS (acquired immunodeficiency syndrome) as a reason laboratory workers leave the profession.[4] A 1987 study, confined to medical technologists, also found a high fear of acquiring AIDS.[5] The purpose of our study was to describe attitudes of medical technologists toward working with AIDS-infected samples.

Methods

(3)   A questionnaire was designed which included 15 questions using Likert rating scales with the response options ranging from strongly agree to strongly disagree. Variables included demographic and institutional factors. Three additional questions dealt with an individual's knowledge of AIDS.

(4)   The questionnaire was distributed to registrants at the 1988 annual meeting of the New Jersey Society for Medical Technology. Of the 295 registrants, 283 were given forms to be filled out anonymously and 212 were returned (75 percent).

Results

(5)   The results showed that fear of AIDS among laboratory workers is common (Table 1). For example, 52 percent agreed with the statement that, despite precautions, it was likely that they could become infected with HIV because of laboratory exposure and 41 percent would like to transfer to a position that required less blood handling. Only 43 percent indicated that they would have chosen the profession knowing they would be handling samples from AIDS patients and one out of four respondents is considering leaving the profession because of a fear of AIDS.

(6)   Medical technologists are clearly experiencing pressure to seek a different career. In 86 percent of those queried, respondents reported that friends and family members expressed concern about their working with HIV samples and 53 percent knew of colleagues who had left the profession because of the possibility that they could acquire the human immunodeficiency virus (HIV).

(7)   On the other hand, there was general satisfaction with employer safety policies. Three out of four felt their employer provided adequate education concerning HIV risk and that adequate safety measures, which lower the risk of HIV transmission, were available. However, less than half felt that their employer offered adequate counseling in the event of an accident.

(8) It was apparent that the AIDS problem had resulted in improved safety practices within the profession. For example, increased reporting of needlestick injuries and the wearing of gloves were reported by 87 percent and 94 percent of the respondents, respectively.

(9) Not surprisingly, those currently working were more inclined to contemplate a career change than people about to enter the field. One

Table 1   Percent of Respondents in Agreement with Survey Questions

Questions	Percent Agreement*
FEAR OF ACQUIRING AIDS QUESTIONS	
I feel I have the right to be informed of HIV+ samples.	96
I believe that fear of acquiring HIV is a major reason for the low enrollments in the MTL and MT schools.	77
Despite precautions, I believe it is likely I could become infected with HIV because of laboratory exposure.	52
In retrospect, I would have chosen the field of medical technology knowing that I would be handling samples from AIDS patients.	43
I would like to remain in the field but would like to transfer to a position that requires less blood handling because of my fear of acquiring AIDS.	41
I am considering leaving the profession because of my fear (and/or my "significant other's" fear) of acquiring HIV in the laboratory.	25
PRESSURE TO LEAVE THE PROFESSION QUESTIONS	
I have had friends or family express concern about my working with HIV positive samples.	86
I know of colleagues who have left the clinical laboratory profession because of their fear (and/or their "significant other's" fear) or acquiring HIV in the laboratory.	53
EMPLOYER SAFETY POLICIES QUESTIONS	
I feel that infection control practices in my lab have improved because of fear of acquiring HIV.	79
I feel my employer provides adequate education on HIV risk.	77
I feel my employer has provided adequate safety measures that lower the risk of HIV transmission in the laboratory.	75
I feel my employer offers adequate counseling in the event of an accident with HIV positive samples.	41
EMPLOYER SAFETY PRACTICES QUESTIONS	
Because of the risk of contracting AIDS, I am more likely to wear gloves today than in the past.	94
Because of the risk of contracting AIDS, I am more likely to report needlestick injuries than in the past.	87
I feel that universal blood precautions will change the way I currently handle samples.	72

*Percent based on a response of strongly agree or agree.

in three of employed medical technologists was thinking about departing the profession because of their fear of AIDS. In contrast, only 13 percent of the students surveyed indicated they were planning to take such a step.

(10)   Further analysis was carried out on the group working in the field to determine if there were any important differences between those considering and those not planning a career change. No important differences were present in respect to age, sex, salary level, marital status, responsibility for dependent children, education level, or working environment (hospital or nonhospital work). Furthermore, the two groups were similar in respect to their knowledge of AIDS (i.e., awareness of the transmission, etiology, and diagnosis of AIDS). The only demographic variable that distinguished the two groups was position in the organization. Of those with supervisory responsibilities, 18 percent were considering a job change versus 38 percent of those without supervisory responsibilities (data available upon request to authors).

Discussion

(11)   These findings suggest that fear of acquiring AIDS contributes to the attrition rate among medical technologists. On a positive note, it was found that medical technologists tend to be satisfied with employer AIDS policies. There was, nevertheless, concern on the part of a majority of workers about the lack of a counseling program in the event of a laboratory accident. Employers can help reduce this anxiety by having counseling programs in place and making sure workers know they exist.

(12)   The survey found that because of AIDS, glove use increased substantially. However, when asked how often they wear gloves, only 46 percent responded that they wore gloves all the time. It therefore appears that laboratory management needs to be more active in motivating their staffs to wear gloves on a regular basis. The

Occupational Safety and Health Administration's mandate for routine glove use, which came out after the survey was completed, places an even greater responsibility on the part of management to see to it that employees use safe practices.

(13) It is also important to note that universal blood precautions, where all samples are to be considered infectious, were in effect when the survey was taken. Still, the overwhelming majority of the respondents (96 percent) felt they had the right to be informed of HIV positive samples. This situation illustrates a common dilemma facing the health care community—a patient's right to privacy and an employee's "right to know."

References

1. Anon: Lab personnel shortage: The growing crisis. Clin Lab Update 1989; 2:1.
2. Myers K, Bronstein R, Vojir C: Why are medical technologists dissatisfied? Lab Med 1982; 13:482–487.
3. Hajek A, Bronstein P: Factors contributing to professional attrition of medical technologists. Lab Med 1982; 13:488–497.
4. Strazybski G: Staffing: Problems and solutions in 19 New England laboratories. Med Lab Observer 1988; 20(11):51–54.
5. Albrecht C, Miller L: Impact of AIDS on clinical laboratorians. Lab Med 1989; 20:187–191.

Acknowledgments

The general results contained in this paper were presented at the following meetings in 1989: International AIDS Conference, American Society for Medical Technologists, and the American Public Health Association.

EXERCISE FOR APPENDIX A

1. What was the authors' stated purpose?

2. In light of the description of the sample in paragraph 4, to what population(s) would you be willing to generalize the results of this study?

3. What percentage of the registrants were given forms to fill out?

4. To be scored as being in agreement with a statement, a subject had to mark one of which two response categories?

5. How many of the subjects (i.e., those who returned the questionnaire) agreed with the statement that, despite precautions, it was likely that they could become infected with HIV because of laboratory exposure.

6. "One out of four" corresponds to what percentage? (See paragraph 5.)

7. "One out of three" corresponds to what percentage? (See paragraph 9.)

8. With which statement in Table 1 did the smallest percentage agree?

9. Were there important differences in marital status between those who were and those who were not planning a career change?

10. The authors report that a larger percentage of those without supervisory responsibilities than those with such responsibilities were considering a job change. Speculate on the reason(s) for this difference.

11. Even though 94 percent of the subjects reported being more likely to wear gloves today, the authors note a problem in this area. What problem do they note?

12. What is your opinion on the authors' decision to combine "strongly agree" with "agree" when summarizing the results in Table 1?

13. In your opinion, do the data support the first statement in paragraph 11? Explain.

14. If you had major funding to conduct a study on the same topic, what changes, if any, would you make in the research methodology?

Notes:

APPENDIX B

DATING VIOLENCE AMONG HIGH SCHOOL STUDENTS*

William Burcky
Nicholas Reuterman
Southern Illinois University

Sondra Kopsky
Granite City Senior High School

(1)   Americans are becoming increasingly aware that physical violence in families is widespread and that it often represents a serious problem for individuals in those relationships. Although accurate data are difficult to obtain, it has been estimated that about two million husbands, and an equivalent number of wives, attack their spouses in any given year (Straus, 1978). In studies conducted to date, researchers have examined not only marital violence (e.g., Straus, Gelles & Steinmetz, 1980; Gelles, 1976) but also parent-child violence (e.g., Stark & McEvoy, 1970; Erlanger, 1974; Gil, 1971), sibling violence (e.g., Steinmetz, 1977), and elderly abuse (e.g., Block & Sinnot, 1980).

(2)   Most of the studies addressing premarital violence have focused primarily on either married or cohabiting couples. Gayford (1978) and Star, Clark, Goetz, and O'Malia (1979) explored the extent to which violence had occurred before marriage. In other research, Hennon (1976) and Yllo and Straus (1980) were concerned with how often cohabiting couples resolve conflict in their relationships through violence. Only one study has examined violence between partners at less committed stages of involvement or at the dating level of the relationship (Makepeace, 1981). Makepeace, using a sample of predominately college freshmen and sophomores, reported that nearly one-fifth (21.1%) of the respondents had experienced at least one direct personal episode of dating violence. Burcky and Roesti (1985) reported similar findings (21.2%) in research involving a population composed of equal numbers of freshmen, sophomore, junior, and senior university students.

---

(3)   In this study, we extended our inquiry to examine the extent of the phenomenon of dating violence among high school students. We defined dating violence as any act perpetrated by the male high school students against the female students that would result in bodily harm or injury. This definition of dating violence was shared with the students completing the survey and was used in the survey instrument for classifying various violent acts. For example, we were interested in factors such as the various types of violence experienced, the stage of the relationship at which the violence occurred, the extent of alcohol and drug abuse, if any, and the individual's actions after abuse by a date.

Method

Sample

(4)   The respondents were 123 high school girls (53 age 15, 19 age 16, 33 age 17, and 11 age 18 to 19) from a large, public high school in the Metro-East area of St. Louis, Missouri. The sample consisted of volunteers from the girls' physical education classes, which were composed of female students from virtually all academic areas. The mean age of the respondents was 16.3 years and the age range was from 15 to 19 years.

The Questionnaire

(5)   Data for this survey were collected by means of a questionnaire, which was an adaptation of the earlier instrument used by Makepeace (1981) in his study. The questionnaire consisted of five separate sections. The first section, biographical information, requested information on age, year in school, family income, academic program followed, grade point average, and involvement in school activities. The second section asked for information on attitudes and opinions regarding dating and dating relationships. The third section requested information on experiences with family discipline and family violence. The fourth section consisted of questions about dating conflicts. Only those respondents who had personally experienced dating violence completed the fifth and final section, in which respondents were asked

for specific details of the incident(s) of violence. Respondents to these questions were asked to indicate the following: (a) in how many such incidents they were involved; (b) with how many different partners; (c) age at time of incident(s); (d) which violent acts were done to them; (e) which violent acts were done by them; (f) their injury level; (g) nature of the relationship; (h) actions before and after the incident; and (i) whether alcohol or drugs had been consumed before the incident by either party.

Results and Discussion

Frequency and Form of Dating Violence

(6) The incidence of violence in the dating relationship was surprisingly prevalent. Of the 123 respondents, 30, or approximately 24%, responded that they had been victims of dating violence on one occasion and 18, or approximately 14.6%, responded they had been victims of dating violence on several occasions. In this study we combined the two groups and reported on them as one group--those involved in dating violence.

Table 1   Experience of High School Girls with Various Types of Dating Violence

Type of violence	Frequency (N = 48)	Percentage
Object thrown at me	14	29.1
Pushed or shoved	32	66.6
Slapped or spanked	22	45.8
Kicked	10	20.8
Bitten	8	16.6
Punched	18	37.5
Struck with an object	7	14.5
Beaten up	6	12.5
Threatened with a knife	3	6.2
Threatened with a gun	3	6.2
Assaulted with a knife	4	8.3
Assaulted with a gun	5	10.4
Other	5	10.4

Note: Some respondents checked more than one response.

(7)   To determine the specific form the violence took, respondents were asked to check terms that best described the violence they experienced. As indicated in Table 1, the most prevalent forms of violence seemed to be acts of physical violence rather than threats of violence. The extremely dangerous and potentially life-threatening forms of violence (e.g., being threatened or assaulted with a knife or gun) are alike in that they were experienced in a relatively small number of cases.

Description of Experience

(8)   The age at the time of the first incident was reported as follows: Approximately 28.5% were 12 to 13 years old; 40.4% were 14 to 15; 28.5% were 16 to 17; and 2.3% were 18 or older. The age of the partners was reported as follows: approximately 35.7% were over 18; 45.2% were 16 to 17; and 16.7% were 14 to 15 years old. When responding to the question, "Was the incident preceded by an argument or disagreement?" approximately 92.3% of the participants said "yes." The major reasons or causes given for the disputes are shown in Table 2.

Table 2   Reasons or Causes for Dating Argument or Disagreement

Reason or cause	Frequency (N = 48)	Percentage
Jealousy	23	47.9
Miscellaneous disagreements	20	41.6
Rejection of partner	11	22.9
Intoxication	11	22.9
Sexual favors	10	20.8
No substantial meaningful answer	9	18.7
Date-activity related	7	14.5
Families	4	8.3
Money related	3	6.2

Note: Some respondents checked more than one response.

(9)   In Table 3 we present data regarding the consumption of alcoholic beverages in the 4 hours before the incident. A drink was defined as either one glass of wine, a bottle of beer, or one mixed drink. These data indicate that the consumption of alcohol was reported in approximately one-third of the incidents. No attempt was made to specify whether the drinking precipitated, accentuated, or caused the episode.

(10)   Respondents and their partners' use of drugs is detailed in Table 4. From the list of drugs, participants were asked to check which ones they or their partners or both used during the four hours before the incident. No attempt was made to quantify the drug usage. Respondents

Table 3   Alcohol Consumption Before Incident

Number of drinks	Respondent's consumption frequency (N = 48)	Percentage	Partner's consumption frequency	Percentage
1 Drink	0	0.0	3	6.2
2-4 Drinks	7	14.5	2	4.1
4-8 Drinks	3	6.2	6	12.5
8 or More drinks	8	16.6	8	16.6
No response	30	62.5	29	60.4

were free to define *usage* based on their own experience. These data indicate that approximately 14% of the respondents and approximately 27% of their partners used drugs during the four hours before the incident.

(11)   As indicated in Table 5, approximately 45% of the relationships in which violence occurred were characterized by the respondents as steady dating. It seems that the more a relationship builds, the greater the possibility for a person to experience violence in that relationship.

Table 4   Drug Usage Four Hours Before Incident

Type of drug	Respondent's usage (N = 48)	Percentage	Partner's usage	Percentage
Marijuana	6	12.5	11	22.9
Amphetamines	0	0.0	1	2.0
Cocaine	1	2.0	2	4.1
Depressants	0	0.0	0	0.0
None used	21	43.7	16	33.3
No response	20	41.6	18	37.5

Table 5   Stage of Relationship in which Violence Occurred

Stage	Frequency (N = 48)	Percentage
First date	6	12.5
Casual dating	7	14.5
Steady dating	22	45.8
Engaged	3	6.2
No response	10	20.8

(12)   The reader might assume that persons who experienced dating violence would terminate the relationship. But five students, or about 10%, responded that they were still seeing the person in the same capacity as they had before the incident. In addition, five students, or approximately 10%, responded that they were more deeply involved in the relationship than they were before the incident occurred. It is interesting that 28 students, or about 58%, broke off the relationship.

Actions After the Incident

(13)   After the incident, 32 respondents (66%) told close friends, four (8%) told parents, four (8%) told brothers or sisters, one (2%) told law enforcement officials, three (6%) told a teacher or counselor, and ten (20%) did not tell anyone.

(14)   In describing the effects of the incident on their emotional state, six students (12%) said the incident had no particular effect on them, 27 (56%) said the incident had upset them, but that it had caused no major trauma and that there were no serious long-term effects, and four (8%) responded that they had experienced substantial trauma and were disturbed about the incident for a long time afterward.

Discussion

(15)   This study reveals that violence is a common occurrence in dating relationships of high school students. The data indicated that almost 40% of those dating experienced some form of violence in the relationship. Although the number is small for those experiencing the more serious forms of violence, we need only to extrapolate these percentages to see the serious implications of the findings. The forms of violence reported in the dating relationships seem to parallel the forms of violence researchers report in marital relationships. This parallel pattern could indicate that the dating period is a period of socialization for establishing marital roles, which include violence toward the spouse as a way to resolve conflict. When we extended the concept of participation in a violent dating relationship and linked it with the nature of violence by parents toward children, we could see that the cycle of violence was being extended into new dating relationships in which these young people were involved. Victimization

as a child increases an individual's tolerance for violence as an adult and, from the early experience, the socialization process comes full circle.

(16)   We found that participants do talk about the incidents of violence and do so in substantial numbers. But an extremely small number tell counselors or talk to them about it. Therefore, we are suggesting that counselors:

1. become aware of the extent of dating violence and understand that it is a common occurrence among high school students,

2. provide professional counseling assistance for those experiencing the trauma of a violent relationship,

3. use their knowledge of dating violence to know when and to whom referrals can be made,

4. develop the necessary community referral network,

5. develop contacts with local medical and social agencies,

6. develop contacts with local abuse centers and law enforcement agencies,

7. make available to students the community's crisis hotline number,

8. coordinate with other school personnel to establish self-help or support groups for those experiencing dating violence, and

9. assist victims of dating violence in making rational decisions about the continuation or termination of the relationship if they so desire.

(17)   Finally, an important consideration for any intervention strategy would be to develop a support system that can provide a pattern of continuous and intermittent relationships. These could play a significant part in maintaining the psychological and physical integrity of the victimized student.

References

Block, M. R., & Sinnot, J. D. (1980). *The battered elder syndrome: An exploratory study.* College Park, MD: Center on Aging.

Burcky, W. D. & Roesti, J. (1985, Summer). Dating violence among college students. *IACD Quarterly,* No. 98.

Erlanger, H. S. (1974). Social class and corporal punishment in child rearing: A reassessment. *American Sociological Review, 39,* 68–85.

Gayford, J. J. (1978). Battered wives. In J. Martin (Ed.), *Violence and the family* (pp. 19–42). New York: Wiley.

Gelles, R. J. (1976). Abused wives: Why do they stay? *Journal of Marriage and the Family, 38,* 659–668.

Gil, D. G. (1971). Violence against children. *Journal of Marriage and the Family, 33,* 644–648.

Hennon, C. B. (1976). *Interpersonal violence and its management by cohabitating couples.* Paper presented at the Western Social Science Association meeting: Tempe, AZ.

Makepeace, J. (1981). Courtship violence among college students. *Family Relations, 30,* 97–102.

Star, B., Clark, C. G., Goetz, K. M., & O'Malia, L. (1979). Psychological aspects of wife battering. *Social Casework, 60,* 479–487.

Stark, R., & McEvoy, J. (1970, November). Middle class violence. *Psychology Today,* pp. 52–65.

Steinmetz, S. K. (1977). *The cycle of violence: Assertive, aggressive, and abusive family interaction.* New York: Praeger.

Straus, M. A. (1978). Wife beating: How common and why? *Victimology, 2,* 443–458.

Straus, M. A., Gelles, R. J., & Steinmetz, S. K. (1980). *Behind closed doors: Violence in the American family.* Garden City, NY: Anchor Books.

Yllo, K., & Straus, M. A. (1980). Interpersonal violence among married and cohabitating couples. *Family Relations, 30,* 339–347.

EXERCISE FOR APPENDIX B

1. In your opinion, have the authors established the importance of this study in the introduction? Explain. (See paragraphs 1, 2, and 3.)

2. Comment on the adequacy of the sample.

3. To two decimal places, what percentage of the 123 subjects reported that they had been victims of dating violence on one occasion?

4. Why do the percentages in Table 1 sum to more than 100 percent?

5. The letter N in Table 1 stands for what word(s)?

6. Is the data in Table 1 based on responses of all 123 respondents? Explain.

7. Which type of violence listed in Table 1 was most frequently reported?

8. Speculate on the advantages of giving each table a number such as "Table 1."

9. In paragraph 7, the authors describe only some of the highlights of Table 1. In your opinion, is this appropriate?

10. Prepare a table to facilitate a comparison of the ages of the respondents and their partners described in paragraph 8. In the first column, list the age groups; in the second, list the percentages of respondents in each age group; and in the third, list the percentages of partners in each age group.

11. Based on your answer to question 10, were the respondents or the partners generally older?

12. Why do the frequencies in Table 2 sum to more than 48?

13. How many of the respondents reported using drugs during the four hours before the incident?

14. In paragraph 11, the authors state that approximately 45 percent of the relationships were characterized as steady dating. Refer to Table 5 to determine a more precise percentage. In your opinion, is the use of such approximations appropriate? Explain.

15. Do you agree with the first sentence of paragraph 15?

16. In paragraph 15, the authors discuss a possible connection between violence in dating and family violence. Are any statistics reported in this article on this connection?

17. Based on this study, are there any suggestions that you would make to school counselors in addition to the nine listed in paragraph 16?

18. If you had major funding to conduct a study on the same topic, what changes, if any, would you make in the methodology and analysis?

Notes:

BELIEFS ABOUT SUICIDE IN AMERICAN AND
TURKISH STUDENTS*

David Lester
Stockton State College

Tulin Icli
Hacettepa University, Turkey

(1)   McIntosh, Hubbard, and Santos (1985) devised an inventory of myths about suicide and explored the extent to which they are held by people in the United States. The myths they described can be more appropriately viewed as beliefs about suicide that may or may not be held in different cultures. The present study explored the extent to which American and Turkish students held these beliefs.

(2)   The American suicide rate from 1979 to 1981 was 12 per 100,000 people per year. The Turkish suicide rate was officially 0.2, but a more realistic estimate may be 1.8 (Isik Sayil, personal communication, 1989). American students are heterogeneous in religious preference, but primarily Christian; Turkish students are primarily Islamic. Because suicide is rarer in Turkey than in the United States, it was expected that people in Turkey would be less familiar with suicidal behavior in friends and family and would read about it less in newspapers and magazines. Thus, their knowledge about suicide should be less accurate.

(3)   The McIntosh (1985) inventory of beliefs about suicide was given to 80 American undergraduates aged 17 to 24 years enrolled in social science courses at an American college (55 women and 25 men; mean age = 20.4 years, SD = 1.5) and to 98 Turkish undergraduates aged 17 to 24 years enrolled in social science courses at a Turkish university (63 women and 35 men; mean age = 20.3, SD = 1.7).

(4)   Turkish students were more likely to agree with the following statements (all chi-square tests have 1 df, and the critical value for significance is 3.84).

---

*The Journal of Social Psychology, 130(6), 825–827, 1990. Reprinted with permission of the Helen Dwight Reid Educational Foundation. Published by Heldref Publications, 4000 Albemarle St., N.W., Washington, D.C. 20016. Copyright 1990.

1. "People who talk about suicide rarely commit suicide" (50.0% vs. 22.5%; chi square = 13.04).

2. "The suicidal person wants to die and feels there is no turning back" (89.8% vs. 53.7%; chi square = 27.62).

3. "Everyone who commits suicide is depressed" (79.6% vs. 33.3%; chi square = 35.56).

4. "There is very little correlation between alcoholism and suicide" (40.8% vs. 20.2%; chi square = 7.63).

5. "If you ask someone directly 'Do you feel like killing yourself?' this will lead them to make a suicide attempt" (13.3% vs. 0.0%; chi square = 9.57).

6. "A suicide attempt means that the attempter will always entertain thoughts of suicide" (58.2% vs. 35.0%; chi square = 8.57).

7. "Suicidal persons rarely seek medical help" (79.6% vs. 58.7%; chi square = 8.18).

8. "All suicides leave a suicide note" (21.4% vs. 1.2%; chi square = 14.75).

9. "Suicide happens without warning" (59.2% vs. 15.0%; chi square = 34.21).

10. "Motives or causes of suicide are readily established" (84.7% vs. 26.6%; chi square = 58.58).

(5) American students were more likely to agree with two beliefs: that the tendency toward suicide is inherited and passed on from one generation to another (24.1% vs. 4.1%; chi square = 13.71) and that oppressive weather (such as rain, humidity, etc.) has been found to be very related to suicidal behavior (71.2% vs. 54.1%; chi square = 4.80).

(6) No significant differences were found for the beliefs that a person who commits suicide is mentally ill, suicide is more common among lower socioeconomic groups, nothing can be done to stop a person attempting suicide once he or she has decided to, and suicides usually occur at night.

(7) Overall, American students agreed with a mean of 4.5 beliefs (SD = 1.9); Turkish students agreed with a mean of 7.3 (SD = 1.8), $t(172)$ = 10.22, $p < .001$. In addition, students were asked to rate the morality of suicide. No significant differences were found in the ratings given by the American and Turkish students. More American students had thought about suicide in the past (47.5% vs. 26.5%; chi square = 7.52),

and more had attempted suicide in the past (10.0% vs. 3.1%), though not significantly so.

(8)   Thus, this study indicated that American undergraduates had been more preoccupied with suicide in the past than Turkish undergraduates, a finding consistent with the official suicide rates of the two nations. However, both groups rated the morality of suicide similarly. Turkish students on the whole agreed with more of the items in the McIntosh inventory of beliefs about suicide, indicating from an American perspective a less accurate knowledge about suicide. However, the items in the McIntosh inventory need to be explored to determine their applicability in Turkish society.

(9)   Previous research has indicated deleterious effects from the dissemination of information about suicide, for example, rises in the suicide rate in the days after a famous suicide (Phillips, 1974). The present study suggests a beneficial effect from the dissemination of information about suicide, namely, less belief in myths about suicide that may impede the effective recognition and helping of suicidal individuals.

References

McIntosh, J. L., Hubbard, R. Q., & Santos, J. F. (1985). Suicide facts and myths. *Death Studies, 9,* 267–281.
Phillips, D. P. (1974). The influence of suggestion on suicide. *American Sociological Review, 39,* 340–354.

EXERCISE FOR APPENDIX C

1. The American suicide rate is how many times higher than the official Turkish rate?

2. According to the authors' prediction, which group should have less accurate information about suicide?

3. The authors did not test to see if there was a significant difference between the means for age for the two groups. Do you believe that they should have done so? Explain.

4. Assuming that the distribution of age is normal, between what two ages does the middle 68 percent of the American subjects lie?

5. Do you believe that the ages of the American students are probably more or less variable than the ages of the whole population of Americans?

6. What *percentage* of the Turkish subjects were women?

7. The authors state that for 1 *df*, the critical value of chi square is 3.84. If you have a statistics textbook, examine the chi-square table and determine the probability associated with this value. Write your finding here.

8. In paragraphs 4 through 6, the authors report on differences for how many beliefs?

9. How many of the differences referred to in question 8 were statistically significant?

10. For the differences referred to in question 8, how many times was the null hypothesis rejected?

11. At the .05 level, for every 100 chi-square tests, how many would you expect to lead to a Type I error (i.e., rejecting the null hypothesis when it is actually true)?

12. Assuming that the distribution of overall scores for Turkish subjects is normal, between what two scores does the middle 68 percent of the Turkish students lie?

13. Assuming that the distribution of overall scores for Turkish subjects is normal, between what two scores does the middle 99 percent of the Turkish students lie?

14. What is the mean difference between the overall scores of American and Turkish subjects (for agreement with the beliefs)?

15. Is the difference between the means referred to in question 14 statistically significant? If yes, at what level?

16. Has the null hypothesis been rejected for the difference referred to in question 14?

17. Do you agree with the implication stated in the last sentence of the article? Explain.

APPENDIX D

EVIDENCE OF THE VALIDITY OF THE PPST FOR NON-TRADITIONAL COLLEGE STUDENTS*

Edward Tokar and Susan deBlois
Youngstown State University

Correlation coefficients and coefficients of determination were calculated for PPST subtest scores for three age groups of college students. PPST reading, math, and writing scores from a sample of 800 university students in teacher education were used for the analysis. In general, correlation coefficients were higher for students 23 years or younger. Coefficients were much lower for students 30 years of age or older. Coefficients of determination suggested that the PPST reading and writing subtest scores account for a sizable amount of variation in college GPA for students 23 and younger (21 and .22), but PPST reading and math accounted for relatively little variation in college GPA for students 30 years or older (.06 and .04). The authors suggest that universities with large enrollments of older, non-traditional students in teacher education programs further examine the validity of using some subtests of the PPST in the decision-making process.

(1)   University campuses nation-wide are experiencing a remarkable change in the types of students enrolling. Non-traditional students are becoming a major influence in all areas of university activity. These larger portions of non-traditional students will have an enormous impact on the way classes are planned, taught, and assessed (Hengstler, 1983; Silling, 1984). Further, prerequisites and requirements for university programs and degrees will be greatly impacted by the influx of older students with life experiences and backgrounds radically different from those of traditional college students (Keller and Switzer, 1983; Silling, 1984). Currently, approximately 42% of undergraduate enrollment is composed of non-traditional students, i.e., incoming students 24 years or older (Sommer, 1989). Clearly, university educators must take into account this growing portion of students when establishing program guidelines and requirements such as entry and exit testing.

---

*Educational and Psychological Measurement, 51, 161–166, 1991. Copyright 1991 by Educational and Psychological Measurement. Reprinted by permission.

(2)   Large-scale testing programs are being used extensively at various levels of the university educational process. Most testing is needed and beneficial for making decisions about large numbers of individuals; however, tests can be of better use when more is known about them. The research on a particular test can increase the understanding of its limits and the boundaries of its usefulness or validity. It is important to investigate a test's parameters for various groups of students. This investigation now needs to include the non-traditional college students in order to determine the degree of validity for each group. An outcome of this process is the determination of the generalizability of the test.

(3)   Since 1986, several states have used the Pre-Professional Skills Test (Educational Testing Service, 1987) to assess the basic skills (reading, math, and writing) of candidates for a larger number of teacher education programs. These tests are generally administered prior to entering a school of education, usually after completion of the sophomore year. In many cases the scores on the Pre-Professional Skills Test (PPST) are a part of the entrance requirements for teacher education programs. Because of the importance of entrance decisions, the validity of these scores must be known. Test validation is partially data derived, with a focus on test scores across groups and settings in order to establish generalizability (Messick, 1989). The purpose of this study was to investigate the characteristics of the PPST in regard to older, non-traditional university students. Through such research, the relevance or validity of the test for non-traditional students can be further identified and defined. In addition, the generalizability of the PPST can be better understood.

(4)   Previous research on the PPST has indicated that it is a moderate predictor of GPA for undergraduate education majors with correlation coefficients of .47, .38, and .43 for reading, mathematics, and writing subtests respectively (Sibert and Ayers, 1989). All three correlations were significant, ($p < .01$), suggesting the three subtests of the PPST were valid for predicting student grade point average. An earlier study by Aksamit, Mitchell, and Pozehl (1987) reported similar correlation coefficients between college GPA and the PPST of .45, .37, and .43 for reading, math, and writing, respectively. In another previous investigation, PPST correlations with freshman English and composite English GPA ranged from .31 to .36 across the three subtests with, of

course, PPST reading the highest (Heard and Ayers, 1988). The focus of the current study is to determine if the PPST is valid for predicting the grade point average of non-traditional university students.

Method

(5)   Subjects for this study were teacher education majors attending a mid-sized public university in an urban setting in the Midwest. Initially, a group of 800 students who had taken the PPST between 1984-87 were identified as the sample of interest. Students were required to take the PPST during their sophomore year and prior to entry in the teacher education program, thereby minimizing the influence of class rank as an extraneous variable. Furthermore, credit for "life experiences" for non-traditional students is not a policy of the university. Approximately one year after the PPST was administered, students' grade point averages were recorded.

(6)   The sample contained 576 women and 224 men. When broken down by age, the sample consisted of 474 students 23 years of age or younger, 136 students between the ages of 24-29, and 190 students between the ages of 30-52. The rationale for trichotomizing on age devolves from the authors' observations of the uniqueness of the three subgroups. Traditional students in Group I have substantially different backgrounds and generally lack the experiences of the non-traditional students. Also, within the non-traditional population, two recognizable subgroups emerged. First, the relatively young non-traditionals in Group II that had initially by-passed college after high school or were returning with a modicum of college course work from a few years earlier. And a second category of non-traditional students, those in Group III, older individuals that were either starting or returning to college after more than a decade. Therefore, determining differential validity of the three age groups was a major interest of the authors.

(7)   After collecting and coding the data, descriptive statistics and correlation coefficients were generated. In addition, coefficients of determination were calculated for each subtest by each group in an effort to explain the amount of variation in GPA that can be accounted for by PPST scores (Mehrens and Lehmann, 1987). SPSS (1975) statistical procedures were employed.

Results

(8)   The means and standard deviations for each subtest of the PPST and college grade point averages are presented for each age group in Table 1. Group I represents students 23 years old or younger; Group II, students ranging in age from 24 to 29; and Group III, students from the ages of 30 to 52. Means for the PPST reading ranged from a standard score of 175.95 for the 23 and lower age group to 177.40 for the 30 and over group. Means for the three groups on the PPST math were remarkably similar, 176.80, 176.67, and 176.95, respectively. Mean performance on the PPST writing subtests ranged from 174.61 for the 24-29 year old group to 176.46 for the 30 and older group. It is interesting to note that those students in the 30 and older group recorded the highest mean performance in two out of three of the PPST subtests. Further examination of the mean grade point averages across the three groups indicated that the 30 and over group appeared substantially higher. Using GPA, a one-way ANOVA resulted in an F ratio of 10.63, which was significant at the .001 level.

Table 1   Means and Standard Deviations of PPST Reading, Math, Writing Subtests, and College GPA for Three Age Groups

Age Group	Group I <24		Group II 24–29		Group III >29	
	M	SD	M	SD	M	SD
PPST-R	175.95	5.60	176.46	5.71	177.40	5.93
PPST-M	176.80	6.64	176.67	7.52	176.95	7.02
PPST-W	175.16	3.81	174.61	3.97	176.46	4.24
GPA	3.04	.41	3.00	.43	3.20	.48

(9)   Correlation coefficients obtained between PPST subtest scores and college grade point averages for the three age groups are presented in Table 2. An inspection of Table 2 reveals that the two lowest coefficients were observed for Group III, 30 years and older, .258 for PPST-R and .218 for PPST-M. In addition, the Group III PPST-M coefficient was not significant when alpha was set at .01. (All other coefficients were significant at the .01 level).

(10)   An examination of the coefficients of determination in Table 2 suggests that a relatively substantial amount of variation in GPA can be accounted for by PPST reading and writing subtest scores for students in Group I. Contrarily, relatively little of the variation in college grade

point average can be accounted for by PPST reading and math subtest scores for Group III, the non-traditional students. The low coefficients of determination for PPST math for the other age groups should also be noted.

Table 2   Correlation Coefficients and Coefficients of Determination for PPST Subtests and College GPA for Three Age Groups

	Group I <24		Group II 24–29		Group III >29	
	r	r^2	r	r^2	r	r^2
PPST-R, GPA	.468	.219	.440	.193	.258	.066
PPST-M, GPA	.312	.097	.260	.067	.218	.047
PPST-W, GPA	.476	.226	.328	.107	.344	.118

Conclusions

(11) The results of this study partly replicate previous research in that correlations of PPST subtest scores with college GPA range from .47 for reading to .37 for math for samples of traditional college students (Aksamit, Mitchell and Pozehl, 1987; Sibert and Ayers, 1989). Correlations of .46, .31, and .47 for PPST reading, math, and writing for students in Group I of the current study were remarkably alike. Similar to previous research, the correlations of PPST math and GPA were the weakest of all subtests across the three age groups (.312, .260, and .218).

(12) When validity coefficients based on the test scores of non-traditional students were examined, other weaknesses emerge. It appears that for students 30 years of age or older, the validity of using PPST reading and math for predicting performance in college is noticeably less than that for other groups, i.e., traditional students. Coefficients of determination were alarmingly low for non-traditional students in Group III for PPST reading and math. However, additional research with similar groups of students across other settings is necessary. The restriction of range of the criterion variable, grade point average, is of concern, especially for Group III.

(13) In summary, the validity of a test score depends on the situation or decision for which the score is used. The test user is the final determiner of the validity and must consider the many consequences of using or not using a score in the decision-making process. The evidence presented in this study suggests that universities with large enrollments

of non-traditional teacher education majors should more carefully examine the efficacy of the PPST in the decision-making process.

References

Aksamit, D., Mitchell, Jr. J. V., & Pozehl, B. J. (1987). Relationships between PPST and ACT scores and their implications for the basic skills testing of prospective teachers. *Journal of Teacher Education.* Nov.–Dec., 48–52.

Educational Testing Service (1987). *Pre-professional Skills Tests score interpretation guide.* Princeton, NJ: Authors.

Heard, S. A. & Ayers, J. B. (1988). Validity of the American College Test in predicting success on the Pre-Professional Skills Test. *Educational and Psychological Measurement, 48,* 197–200.

Hengstler, D. D. (1983). Androgogy on public universities: Understanding adult education needs in the 1980's. (ERIC Document Reproduction Service No. ED 246 777).

Keller, J. E. & Switzer, D. E. (1983). The evaluation of teacher effectiveness: The implications of different perspectives of traditional and nontraditional students. (ERIC Document Reproduction Service No. ED 238 064).

Mehrens, W. A. & Lehmann, I. J. (1987). *Using standardized tests in education* (4th ed.). White Plains, New York: Longman, Inc.

Messick, S. (1989). Meaning and values in test validation: The science and ethics of assessment. *Educational Research, 6,* 5–11.

SPSS. (1975). *SPSS user's guide.* New York: McGraw-Hill.

Sibert, P. C. & Ayers, J. B. (1989). Relationships between scores from the ACT, PPST, NTE, ACTCOMP, and GPA. *Educational and Psychological Measurement, 49,* 945–949.

Silling, M. A. (1984). Student services for adult learners. (ERIC Document Reproduction Service No. ED 253 809).

Sommer, R. (1989). Educating adults and non-traditional students: Some implications of the changing demographics in freshman composition. (ERIC Document Reproduction Service No. ED 303 810).

EXERCISE FOR APPENDIX D

1. In the first paragraph, how are non-traditional students defined?

2. For what words does PPST stand?

3. In the study by Sibert and Ayers (1989), which subtest had the lowest correlation with GPA?

4. What *percentage* of the subjects were between the ages of 30 and 52?

5. Which measure of central tendency is reported in Table 1?

6. Which measure of variability is reported in Table 1?

7. What was the mean score on PPST-M for subjects who ranged in age from 24 to 29?

8. Which group was least variable in their GPAs?

9. Was the null hypothesis for the differences in mean GPAs rejected? Explain.

10. For subjects aged 24 or less, the weakest relationship was between which two variables?

11. Describe in words (not numbers) the strength and direction of the relationship between PPST-M and GPA for Group III.

12. In paragraph 10, the authors mention the coefficients of determination. What symbol in Table 2 stands for these coefficients?

13. Which coefficient in Table 2 was not statistically significant at the .01 level?

14. If the authors had chosen the .05 level to test for significance, would it be more likely or less likely that the coefficient referred to in question 13 would have been significant? Explain.

15. What *percentage* of the variation in GPA is accounted for by the variation in PPST-M for Group III?

16. Speculate on the meaning of the term "validity coefficients," as it is used in paragraph 12.

17. Do you agree with the summary in the last paragraph of the article? Explain.

Notes:

Notes:

Notes:

Notes: